DEVELOPING IN UNDERDEVELOPMENT IN NIGERIA: HAND OF CORRUPTION

DEVELOPING IN UNDERDEVELOPMENT IN NIGERIA: HAND OF CORRUPTION

Akinyetun Tope Shola

CONTENTS

List of Tables and Figures

Preface

Introduction   1

Meaning of Corruption   2

Typology of Corruption   7

Theoretical Perspectives   26

Causes of Corruption   32

Incidence of Corruption in Nigeria   38

Costs and Consequences of Corruption in Nigeria   44
Corruption and Underdevelopment Interface:
The Case of Nigeria   59
Analyses of Legal Frameworks of the Fight against Corruption in Nigeria   70

Curbing Corruption in Nigeria   86

Bibliography   96

LIST OF TABLES AND FIGURES

Table 1: Forms of Corruption

Table 2: Typology of Corruption Based on Actor Categories

Table 3: Identification of the Provider of Corruption

Table 4: Corruption - Framework for Defense

Table 5: Nigeria's Corruption Perception Index Rankings, 1996-2014

Table 6: Annual Basic Salaries of Nigerian Lawmakers

Table 7: EFCC Corruption Cases

Table 8: Incidence of Poverty in Nigeria

Table 9: Relative Poverty by Sector - Urban and Rural (%)

Table 10: Trends in Poverty by Geo-Political Zone (%)

Table 11: Percentage of Unemployment Rate

Table 12: Graduates Unemployment Rates 2003-2011

Figure 1: Forms of Corruption - A Simple View

PREFACE

The absence of social amenities as well as the prolonged challenges in social issues, majorly bothering on poverty, inequality and unemployment, has been on the rise in Nigeria. The potency inherent in her human and natural resources has thus not been fully exploited. This jinx of underdevelopment has not been broken and has invariably left development in the country a mirage. The merry-go-rounding around development and underdevelopment [as it were] has earned the country the status of a 'Third World Nation' characterized by pervasive poverty, disease pandemic, hunger and malnutrition, unemployment, child mortality, low life expectancy, illiteracy, unequal trade exchange; lack of initiatives etc. Categorically, Nigeria's development in underdevelopment has been blamed on corruption stemming from the notion of 'national-cake' and resulting in economic-hemorrhage.

The need to expose the 'culprit'-corruption, has driven me to embark on this academic voyage so as to provide transfusion for the country and resuscitate 'her' from the corruption-induced-coma; after all, the effects of the cankerworm are far-reaching; involving the economic, political and social realms. I strongly believe that readers of this academic work will not only be exposed to the meaning of corruption or how it has become so attractive in present day, they will also be informed about the cost and consequences of corruption, the various forms in which it is perpetuated and scholarly opinions about the concept. At the same time, readers will be equipped with the knowledge of how corruption has further exposed Nigeria to underdevelopment with particular references to poverty, inequality and unemployment, as well as ways in which the menace can be curbed.

In the course of putting this work together, I have learnt a lot about the dynamics of development and underdevelopment and how wide and thin the line of demarcation is; depending on the perspective and approach. I have gained insights on how intense the 'practice' of corruption is in Nigeria and how easily it has crossed the threshold of religion, family, academics and other units of socialization. The journey has not been stress-free especially considering the fact that many authors treat the effect of corruption on economic growth and development disjointedly. This work relied majorly on secondary data from works of scholars and authorities in the area of African Studies, State Structure and Development Studies, I can assure the readers that the works of these authors are brilliant.

I hereby acknowledge all authors whose works I cited as a basis for my argument even though I doubt I did adequate justice to that in the bibliography. I am sure this work would have been too hollow and pedestrian without their strands of thought.

I also acknowledge the members of Akinyetun family both home and abroad for their love. So also members of CCCSP AOCOED and CSP UNIBEN for their prayers. Thank you everyone.

I finally wish to urge the reader to read with an open mind and criticize constructively.

AKINYETUN, Tope Shola

DEVELOPING IN UNDERDEVELOPMENT IN NIGERIA: HAND OF CORRUPTION

1.   INTRODUCTION

Nigeria, a West African country with a population of over 170 million people dispersed across 36 states, 1 federal capital territory and 774 local government areas thereby governed by 811 levels of government, is richly endowed with vast natural resources which includes but is not limited to gold, iron-ore, limestone, coal, lead/zinc, oil and gas and bitumen. Indeed until recently when Nigeria fell behind Angola, Nigeria has been the largest oil producing nation in Africa with oil selling for an average of $77/Barrel in 2010, $117/Barrel in 2011, $113/Barrel in 2012, $112/Barrel in 2013, $111/Barrel in 2014 before facing a hit in 2015 to $48/Barrel. The foregoing gives the impression that the country and her citizens are in affluence and that the country should be among the developed nations of the world. Yet, what is obtainable is more than a reverse of this conjecture and begs the question of what has been happening to the major indices of development; reduction in the rate of unemployment, poverty and inequality. A quick survey of these social concerns will paint a clearer picture of the level of development [or otherwise] in Nigeria. Unemployment has soared higher in the last decade ditto for poverty which presently is witnessed in all spheres of the country with an average Nigerian reported to be living below $1 per day. Due to poverty, the relative few who can afford 3 meals are not certain of 3 squared meals as the square-*ness* which means it is balanced is seriously missing. Meanwhile inequality on the other hand is a motif of the Nigerian society wherein the gap between the rich and the poor is as that between the sky and the dry land; indeed there is social alienation in all corners of the state.

1.1   MEANING OF CORRUPTION

Corruption has been explained as the reason for continuous dive in underdevelopment in Nigeria and the eventual increase in the said social issues; unemployment, poverty and inequality. With the epidemic wave of corruption in the country, it is not surprising that development seems far off. In other words, central to the explaining of underdevelopment in Nigeria is corruption.

1

The level of corruption in Nigeria is deep to the extent that not engaging in corruption is like suffering from social leprosy or better still such a person is an outcast or an alien. Nigerians, demand, glorify, justify, celebrate and ancestralize corruption. Indeed if you hold any political, executive, judicial, academic or bureaucratic office and you do not engage in corruption, you are seen as a nitwit.

Corruption in Nigeria has gone beyond greed, poverty, and wickedness, but is now psychotic, hence the call by some for a medically-certified-corruption-brain-surgeon or psychiatrist. Corruption is seen as a business in Nigeria, it is a way of life, a form of acculturation, a way of socializing, a source of pride, prestige, status and a sharp way out of poverty, hence its institutionalization. It has become another form of political culture and socialization. The largesse from corruption can be better understood in light of the rush of Nigerian state actors into politics and their attitude towards power capturing and sustaining. Indeed, corruption in Nigeria is not only political, economic, or social, it is exists in the three domains; cognitive, affective and evaluative.

Corruption impedes a state's ability to use its available resources to progressively achieve the full realization of [socio-economic] rights because national resources are instead diverted into the pockets of public officials, or because development aid is mismanaged, misused or misappropriated. Corruption promotes wrong choices and competition does not keep down prices; rather, the competition is about the size of the bribe. Corruption is costly. At a macro fiscal level, the state loses revenue from abuse of taxes, customs levies, licensing fees and traffic fines. It also leads to high spending due to corruption loadings and fronting on state contracts. The distortion of policy and resource and resource allocations increases inefficiency. Corruption also impacts on investment and growth, especially in countries in need of foreign productive capital. Foreign investors, especially those likely to make long-term contributions to development, are discouraged, although some investors looking to make fast profits through questionable schemes may try their luck. Furthermore, corruption in aid programmes means less for those most in need and may compromise future funding.

2

Corruption is costly, not only for the general public but mainly for the poor as resources are diverted away from them. Service delivery and related policy is distorted if allocation and prioritization are determined by bribes. It means a few benefit at the expense of many which reinforces existing socioeconomic inequality and makes the poor even more vulnerable. Structural inequality leads to many being denied access to education, to information, and therefore to knowledge about their rights that could enable them to challenge abuse of power. Thus, it has been argued that the roots of corruption lie in the unequal distribution of resources in a society. Corruption thrives on economic inequality. Economic inequality provides a fertile breeding ground for corruption–and, in turn, it leads to further inequalities.

Corruption, because of its pervasiveness in many countries in Africa South of the Sahara, is detrimental to social, political, and economic development in a variety of ways. A program of sustainable development is contingent on several conditions, including principled and purposeful leadership; prudent, rational and far-sighted decision-making; and optimum use of available resources. Corruption tends to undermine all these conditions in terms of public cynicism and erosion of confidence on corrupt leadership; irrational, short sighted and ill motivated decision; and squandering of resources on ill-advised or unsuitable projects. The result has developmental stagnation, poverty, the cynicism of the political leadership, and disillusionment and hopelessness on the part of the masses and the deprived. Corruption is multi-faceted affecting all spheres of our socio-economic life and politics. Both the legislature, the Executive, the Judiciary, the private sector, the civil society are all involved.

A study by the Council for the Advancement of the South African Constitution (CASAC) points out that corruption is therefore an antithesis to democracy and the rule of law. Corruption diverts resources that are needed to improve the lives of citizens to enrich a few, at great cost to many. Corruption prevents the state from fulfilling its constitutional obligations, erodes the legitimacy of our democratic government and subverts the rule of law. It gnaws away at the ethical fabric of our society, and stifles economic growth. It has a powerful negative effect on foreign investment by destroying investor confidence. Corruption is any form of reciprocal behavior or transaction where both the power/office holder can respectively initiate the inducement of each other by some rewards to grant (illegal) preferential treatment or favour against the principles and interest of specific organization (or public) within the society. Corruption is defined by the World Bank and Transparency International (TI) as the misuse of public office for private gain. As such, it involves the improper and unlawful behaviour of public-service officials, both politicians and civil servants, whose positions create opportunities for the diversion of money and assets from government to themselves and their accomplices. Corruption distorts resource allocation and government performance.

The Encyclopedia of Social Sciences defines corruption as the misuse of public power for private profit. Like the definition by Transparency International, this one also focuses on the public sector. The Corrupt Practices and other related offences Act, 2000 defines corruption to include bribery, fraud and other related offences like gratification. The Act gave a very wide definition of gratification to mean among other things the offer or promise or receipt or demand of money, donation, gift, loan, fee, reward, valuable security, property or interest in property with the intent to influence such a person in the performance or non-performance of his/her duties. Although the definition of corruption by the Act is vague, it gives a wide ranging definition of gratification. The International Monetary Fund defined corruption as "abuse of authority or trust for private benefit: and is a temptation indulged in not only by public officials but also by those in positions of trust or authority in private enterprises or non-profit organizations". The ICPC Act states that corruption includes bribery, fraud and other related offences. No doubt, the scope of corruption is elastic and includes: use of one's office for pecuniary advantages, gratification, influence peddling, insincerity in advice with the aim of gaining advantage, less than a full day's work for a full day's pay, tardiness and slovenliness etc. Corruption is defined as "an arrangement that involves an exchange between two parties (the demander and the supplier) which (i) has an influence on the allocation of resources either immediately or in the future; and (ii) involves the use or abuse of public or collective responsibility for private ends".

The African Union Convention on Preventing and Combating Corruption and Related Offences lists acts of corruption to include:

a. The solicitation or acceptance, directly or indirectly by a public official or any other person, of any goods of monetary, or other benefit, such as a gift, favour, promise or advantage for himself or herself or for another person or entity, in exchange for any act or omission in the performance of his or her public functions;

b. The offering or granting, directly or indirectly, to a public official or any other person of any goods of monetary value, or other benefit, such as a gift, favour, promise or advantage for himself or herself or for any person or entity, in exchange for any act or omission in the performance of his or her public functions;

c. The offering or granting, directly or indirectly, to a public official or any other person for the purpose of illicitly obtaining benefits for himself or herself or for a third party;

d. The diversion by a public official or any other person, for purposes unrelated to those for which they were intended, for his own or her own benefit or that of a third party, of any property belonging to the State or its agencies, to an independent agency, or to an individual, that such official has received by virtue of his or her position;

e. The offering or giving, promising, solicitation or acceptance, directly or indirectly, of any undue advantage to or by any person, who directs or works for, in any capacity, a private sector entity, for himself or herself or for anyone else, for him or her to act or refrain from acting, in breach of his or her duties;

f. The offering, giving, soliciting or accepting directly or indirectly, or promising of any undue advantage to or by any person who asserts or confirms that he or she is able to exert any improper influence over the decision making of any person performing functions in the public or private sector in consideration thereof, whether the undue advantage is for himself or herself or for anyone else, as well as the request, receipt or the acceptance of the offer or the promise of such an advantage, in consideration of that influence, whether or not the influence is exerted or whether or not the supposed influence leads to the intended result;

g. Illicit enrichment

h. The use or concealment of proceeds derived from any of the acts referred to in this article; and

i. Participation as a principal, co-principal, agent, instigator, accomplice or accessory after the fact, or in any other manner in the commission or attempted commission of, in any collaboration or conspiracy to commit, any of the acts referred to in this article. The Corrupt Practices and other related offences Act 2000 lists offences, which are punishable by the Act to include among other things gratification by an official, corrupt offers to public officers, corrupt demand by persons, fraudulent acquisition of property, fraudulent receipt of property, making false statement or return, gratification by and through agents, bribery of public officers and using position for gratification.

2.   TYPOLOGY OF CORRUPTION

Corruption is not a one-size-fits-all, but it manifests itself in different shades and colours. Despite the fact that corruption exists in both public and private spaces, there are generic types of corruption that are found in either of these spaces. Corruption manifests itself in three types as presented by the USAID. The pair of corruption under each category belongs to the far end of the pendulum for each pair as follows:

Systematic versus Sporadic Corruption

In this category, systematic corruption applies to a situation where the practice has sunk its roots into a system such that it has become the accepted normal behaviour. Such a situation comes about after repeated indulgence in corrupt practices such that the behaviour becomes imbedded within individuals and is viewed as a normal practice. On the contrary, sporadic corruption is an intermittent form of corruption which is not an everyday practice but manifests itself as an exception. While systematic corruption would be intentional, sporadic corruption is not.

Organized versus Disorganized Corruption

These two forms of corruption involves either groups of organized people purposively organized for corrupt practices or isolated cases of corrupt practices. In organized corruption, a number of officials and systems within an organization partake in and share the gains from routine corrupt practices. Partakers to such practice share a common vision and purpose and act collectively for their collective benefit. On the other hand, disorganized corruption takes place opportunistically on a case-by-case basis and each case is unique. Partakers to such type of corruption do not share a common vision and purpose and operate in an individualistic basis without involving collective and concerted effort by a group of organized individuals.

Grand versus petty

These two forms of corruption allude to the size or magnitude of the corruption. Grand corruption refers to large scale abuse and misuse of power while petty corruption is characterized by small-scale abuse and misuse of power. In the latter form of corruption the public is exposed to corrupt individuals who subvert their mandate to serve for personal gain.

Table 1: Forms of Corruption

Type	Status of Main Perpetrator	Enabling Means	Usual Motive	Victims of Corruption
Political corruption	-Chief Executives -Other Political Office Holders	-political power -economic power -social power	-to gain or retain political power -to victimize	-ideals and values of the polity -political opponents
Economic and commercial corruption	-businessmen -contractors -consultants	-economic power -political and social connections	-to make more profits and money	-the generality of tax payers and other citizens
Administrative and professional corruption	-highly place civil servants and executives of parastatals	-Administrative authority - technicality, exclusivity and -professional such as lawyers, doctors, engineers, university teachers etc.	-material wealth - cultivation of political and social connections autonomy of the professions	-the generality of tax payers and other citizens -consumers of the professions
Organized corruption	-political, economic, social and bureaucratic elites -high echelons of control agencies	-influential connections to information sources -control and enforcement authority	Money and material wealth	-government treasure -private individuals
Working class corruption	-artisans -junior and intermediate staff -market women and men	-technicalities of occupational skill -ignorance and carelessness and acquiescence of the public	Money and material wealth to make ends meet	Consumers of goods and services

Categorization of Corruption

Corruption can be categorized from different perspectives. Corruption can be classified according to how it is carried out in relation to established rules in administration. There are two types of corruption in this regard. The first is done "according to the rule" where an official receives private gain for doing what he/she is paid to do. The second is done "against the rule" where an official is paid bribe to give services that he/she is prohibited from providing.

Pedersen and Johannsen (2008) developed a model to analyze the different forms of corruption (Figure 1).

Figure 1: Forms of corruption – a simple view

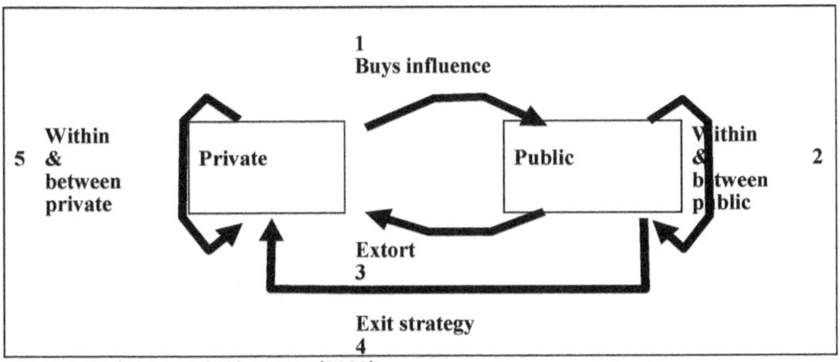

Source: Pedersen and Johannsen (2008)

Corruption can be active or passive taking into consideration who is the person that has the power of decision making or to whom is requested. Corruption also can be private among particular individuals and public corruption that takes place in the public sphere of politics and government administration. A basic categorization considers political corruption, economic corruption and public administration corruption.

Political corruption

Political corruption results in gaining political power. There is political corruption when the behaviors deviate from the principles that guide politics and policies, adapting decisions with abuse of power, which means that the private interests displace the public and common interests. Power is used to service the private interest.

Economic corruption

Economic corruption can be defined as the sacrifice of the principal's interest for the agent's interest. Economic corruption results in making profits. Economic corruption has implications of determining the loss of income, how and how much for the principal, the agent, the state, the consumer, the economy, etc.

Public administration corruption

In the administrative corruption the behaviors of public agents neglect the principles of efficiency, truthfulness and rightfulness. Public administration corruption results in transfer of public benefits to private benefits taking advantage of the entrusted power, as for example, in the form of nepotism that results in the transfer of benefits from society to family members. Taking into consideration the magnitude of corruption, the type of corruption can be grand corruption and petty corruption. According to the depth, corruption can be individual and systemic. Other typology of corruption also considers commercial scale illegal logging, and legal logging but contributions paid to gain access to concessions of resources. Some examples of forms of corruption are bribery, collusion, embezzlement of public funds and theft, fraud, extortion, abuse of discretion, favoritism, clienteles, nepotism, the sale of government property by public officials, patronage, etc.

Bribery is the most widespread form of corruption driven by lucrative profits and the giving of some form of benefit to unduly influence some action or decision on the part of the recipient or beneficiary. Bribery provides incentives for over-regulation and overbureaucratization of procedures. Bribery is likely representing the transfer of a portion of rent to government officials. Bribery is committed when a public servant is offered, promised, or granted an in return for an action already carried out or is to be expected. Bribery can be initiated by the person soliciting the bribe or the person offering the bribe. The benefits may vary from money or other valuables to less tangible ones such as inside information or employment. Bribery as illegal action of corrupt relationships is conducted between the involved expending time and resources to keep their secret out of risk and instability that harms reputations when a word ultimately leaks.

10

Jurists have developed a typology of bribery. Bribery as a form of corruption can be active or passive, in public office or in business relationships. The different types of bribes have different impact depending of the level that can be from tempting of individual politicians to political landscape conservation of factions and parties, from an extraordinarily high one time payments for a specific purpose to impact donations to influence future decisions.

There are some circumstances that are conducive to bribery, including the amount of discretion that civil servants are able to exercise, a legal system that fails to punish bribery, and private companies that are willing to pay the costs of doing business. Bribery also can be a characteristic of the vacuum of political power. Bribery becomes a part of the normal course of business after a firm makes some payments because bureaucrats worldwide expected similar treatment. Bribes may be paid on a case-by-case basis or as part of an ongoing relationship. Consequently, the bribery estimate between firms and the public sector does not cover every form of corruption, such as embezzlement. The estimate of worldwide bribery does not include the extent of other forms of corruption such as embezzlement of public funds from central and local budgets, or from theft or misuse of public assets.

Collusion. Some behaviors of corrupt collusions lead to the subversion of the flow of information within an economic, societal or political unit. Contractual collusion between two parties A and B, to convert a non-tradeable contractual condition such as safety conditions into a tradeable, earns them a rent over and above normal profits. Corruption can be collusive in nature where individuals escape official regulations or sanctions by paying bribes to officials. Because of a contractual collusion, consumer C suffers an externality through an unperceived drop in safety.

Embezzlement and theft are forms of corruption characterized by the taking or conversion of money, property or other valuables for personal benefit. Embezzlement often happens by colluding with the subcontractors who are employed for performing some services such as the maintenance work. Officials can have a source of revenue if they embezzle money from the budget for financing the maintenance work, for example. Embezzlement and theft involve the taking of property by someone to whom it has been entrusted. In the aggregate, this represents embezzlement of state revenues of the first order. Embezzlement, fraud, enrichment in office, favoritism, clienteles, nepotism, simony etc., are forms of corruption and misdemeanor in office. The misuse of authority and power for personal benefits can be embezzlement, enrichment in office, fraud, favoritism and nepotism. Although it is a very serious form of corruption, there are no worldwide estimates of embezzled funds, because it is difficult to have an estimate for the worldwide extent of embezzlement in the public sector from central and local budgets.

Fraud consists of the use of misleading information to induce someone to turn over the property voluntarily, such as the case of misrepresenting the amount of people in need of a particular service. Also other typical fraudulent practice is the sales-buy relationships between public and private sectors. It is well known the form of corruption based on fraudulent sales of second hand or surplus equipment, but when the buyer is the public sector there is no attempt to include the extent of fraud within the private sector.

Extortion involves coercive incentives such as the use of threat of violence or the exposure or damaging information in order to induce cooperation. The typical extortion is a small scale bribery such to pay to pass security check points or the soliciting of money by low level official where the office holders can be either the instigators or the victims of extortion. Under the form of extortion clients and consumers of government or public services have to pay bribes in addition to the official price, license, permits, and access to facilities, etc. As a form of political corruption prevalent in many settings, politicians and public officials make extortions to smaller and weaker firms.

Abuse of discretion is concerning abuses and corrupt government agency practices for private gain without external inducement or extortion. The administrative structure system functioning from high national levels through to the local levels is established by corrupt governments premised on enabling state agents to comprehensively abuse citizen

12

rights for their own personal benefits and in complicity that of their partners and extended network. Some politicians and public officials abuse their political power to capture natural resource rents in such sectors as the mining sector, for example.

In some societies, the combination of acceptance in the face of entrenched systems of abuse has become the norm. Human rights abuses are associated with economic exploitation taking place in areas under the control of the armed opposition and their foreign backers. The history of colonial societies during the last centuries has provided ample examples of how the unprincipled exploitation of natural resources can give rise to human rights abuses also and it has demonstrated how corruption or the mismanagement of natural resources can undermine a country's development and hence the social and economic rights of their citizens. Government officials, who are the perpetrators of human rights abuses shielded on the impunity of the rule of law, address the endemic problems of corruption and resource and financial mismanagement to gain benefits exploited as effectively as possible to the tangible benefit of the population as a whole.

At the global and international levels, the comprehensive and systematic abuse of power and authority on global and international laws, standards and norms for all aspects of national level are striking. Patterns of such abuses are usually associated with bureaucracies in which broad individual discretion is created and few oversights or accountability structures are present. Also these abuses of office's discretion are related to complex decision-making rules which are capable to neutralize the effectiveness of such structures.

Abuses of natural public resources, asset confiscation and forfeiture by governments, law enforcement agencies and political appointees are so egregious that the assets are sold in fake actions to relatives and friends of prominent politicians, party hacks, etc. at bargain prices. The ruling political parties are potentially more likely to have members who are in positions where they would be able to abuse public resources. Common types of abuses in privatization of state owned enterprises are bankrupting them and assigning a lower value than the real estimate.

Favoritism, gift-giving, nepotism, clienteles and financing networks of cronyism and patronage

as forms of corruption involve abuse of discretion, although the act is governed not by the direct self-interest of the corrupt individual, but by some less tangible affiliation, such as advancing the interest of family or nepotism, a political party, or of an ethnic, religious or other grouping. The incidence of corruption practices such as gift-giving and nepotism increased "not as much the result of the deviance of behavior from accepted norms as it is the deviance of norms from the established patterns of behavior. Citizens follow informal institutions and rules and corrupt practices such as bribery and nepotism to obtain public benefits, goods and services, where they are signaled by mistrust in the transparency and efficaciousness of state institutions. There are some countries where public sector institutions are historically based on patronage and nepotism rather than merit, and the consequences may be different. Nepotism increases public employment as a substitute for deficient public works. Per capita higher income of individuals relieves family obligations and lowers the incidence of nepotism. Nepotism subverts laws promoting equity in the workforce and usually increasing the gender inequality.

Other form of corruption is clienteles where are exchanged votes for managerial decisions related to individual and collective goods, mainly for infrastructure o equipment such as roads, schools, etc. Ethnic based patron-clienteles and prebendalism, gives officeholders and bureaucrats the opportunity to make official decisions as vehicles for rewarding political support and contribute to personal or clan enrichment. Well established networks of clienteles always as the result of inequality and in-group trust, have to be controlled more intensively.

Improper political contributions are payments made in an attempt to unduly influence present or future activities by a party or its members when they are in office. To distinguish this from legitimate political contributions is very difficult. The political economy literature explains distortions due to the influence of special political interest groups. Some forms of corruption and venal behaviors can be categorized as improper political contributions such as acceleration or facilitation fees for the provision of goods, services or the divulging of information; information altering fees to subvert the flow of truth and complete information and the selling of permits; income supplement of the provider without affecting the real world; relocation fees are benefits paid to affect the allocation of economic resources, material wealth and the rights such as concessions, licenses, permits, tenders awarded, assets privatized, etc.

The perception of corruption influences the political and economic behavior of citizens in actions such as voting or investment decisions. The term 'the grabbing hand' describes rent-seeking governments which are constrained only by the political and economic institutions in their countries. Political rights consistently had no significant effect on corruption.

Examples of some typologies of corruption
Corruption typology of Roebuck and Barker (1974)
Roebuck and Barker postulates an empirical typology of police corruption derived from a content analysis of the literature published during 1960-1972 and the police work experience. Police corruption is analyzed as a form of organizational deviance hinging primarily on informal police peer group norms. The types of police corruption delineated are:

Corruption of authority
Kickbacks
Opportunistic theft
Shakedowns
Protection of illegal activities
The fix
Direct criminal activities, and
Internal payoffs

15

These types are analyzed along the dimensions of acts and actors, norm violations, support from peer group, (organizational degree of deviant practices, and police department's reactions. Contradictions among formal norms, informal norms, and situational rules are indicated.

Corruption typology of Heidenheimer (1989)

Heidenheimer distinguishes three different evaluations of corruption in society:

White corruption: Corrupt behavior is coded tolerantly. This is typically the case in traditional family based system as well as in patron-client based systems.

Grey corruption: Corruption is regarded with some opprobrium. Corruption is reprehensible in public moral standards, but the affected persons are widely missing a consciousness of doing wrong. This is typical for modern constitutional states and states in transition towards democratic political culture.

Black corruption: Corruption is generally regarded as severe violation of community moral and legal norms. This is characteristic for modern democratic media societies.

Corruption typology of Alemann (1995)

Corruption in societies is inevitable, being a part of informal politics or shadow politics is ranging from a grey area of completely normal informal agreements and regulations to the black area of illegal and unlawful corruption and organized crime. Corruption is the extreme black side of a scale of informal politics, or shadow politics. At what point grey behavior of informal politics turns to black corruption, is extremely difficult to fix, such as for example, a smile is not a bribe.

Alemann proposed the following types of corruption in his typology:

- low level corruption
- top level corruption or
- petty corruption
- routine corruption
- aggravated corruption

Corruption defined as a breach of contract with externalities, constituting at least a three agent game which can derive in the typology of contracts private, public, and political. Corruption is always a process of exchange between two persons groups: The corrupter (A), who has economic resources at his disposal, and the corruptible person (corruptee B), who has power resources at his disposal.

Corruption can be conceptualized as a model of a cycle of at least seven steps. The exchange logic of corruption is formed by the following 7 components of corruption.

1. The buyer (the person offering the bribe: the corrupter) wants
2. a rare good (an order, license, or position) which
3. the seller (the person to be bribed: the corruptee) can assign. The latter receives
4. an additional incentive (money or payment in kind) for the assignment above the normal price. The corruptee thereby
5. violates generally accepted moral standards and
6. damages the interests of a third party or competitor and/or the public interest.
7. Therefore corruption is hidden and concealed.

3 Way Corruption typology of Punch (2000)

Punch (2000) defines corruption as doing something against the officer's duty in exchange for money or gifts from an external corruptor. The 3 way typology of corruption, misconduct and crime modeled by Punch distinguishes between 3 categories of police deviance:

corruption is the conventional understanding of taking something (such as a bribe), against your duty, to do or not to do something, as an exchange from an external corruptor.

misconduct involves police breaking their own internal rules and procedures.

police crime describes behavior such as using excessive violence, drug dealing, theft and burglary, sexual harassment, and violating a person's rights.

Punch provides more detail on the nature of those incidents and who is involved. The typology describes the purposes defining what we are looking at and provide a useful framework for further exploring other causal factors such as personality, background, social dynamics, as well as tailoring prevention efforts.

Typology of corruption in privatization of state owned companies Tserendondov (2001)
Analyzing the case of corruption in privatization of state owned enterprises in Mongolia, Tserendondov develops a typology of corruption which provides a framework of reference for dealing with individual corruption in different contexts of privatization:
-Taking state assets without competition and misusing public funds for their own benefit.
-State individuals, groups, or firms using their current position and authority to influence the formation of privatization laws and other government policies.
- Bankrupting state owned enterprises and assigning a lower value than the real estimate have become common types of abuses in privatization.
- The law was breached by privatizing property into the ownership of unfairly authorized people or by privatizing it based on a low appraisal of property value.
Holmes (2006) is optimistic about the possibility of building a comprehensive hierarchical typology of corruption which is a challenging task for methodological and empirical reasons.

Corruption typology of Miller (2003)
Miller sustains that officers are vulnerable to bribes when they feel let down by their job and develop a dual typology of corruption:
– *Individual* vs Organized, internally *networked*

Corruption typology of Skogan and Meares (2004)
Proactive vs reactive
– *Personal gain vs organizational gain* ('noble-cause' corruption)

Rasma (2005) presented her typology of corruption and how the combination of systemic inadequacies and a culture of impunity have created an environment in which corruption can flourish unchecked.

Corruption typology of Pedersen and Johannsen (2008)

Pedersen and Johannsen (2008) have developed a typology of corruption based on actor categories

Table 2: A typology of corruption based on actor categories

		The purchaser	The provider
Petty corruption	Day-to-day corruption	Individual citizens	Individual providers of public services– health personnel, police
	Administrative malpractice	Individual economic actors–firms etc.	Public control and licensing agencies
Grand corruption	Political state capture	Collective economic actors– interest organizations Individual economic actors	Politicians– individuals and political parties

Source: Pedersen and Johannsen (2008)

A typology of corruption can be developed as an analytical tool based on different levels of severity of state capture, administrative corruption and other determinants associated with the institutional capacity of the state.

Corruption typology of Baker

Ray Baker´s typology of corruption considers the following forms of corruption based on the actors: Traditional government corruption, criminal corruption, entrepreneurial governmental corruption. Political influence, state capture and administrative corruption are phenomena at the interface between the public sphere in which political actors, public administrators and civil servants operate and relate to actors of the private sphere, persons, firms, nongovernmental organizations, civil society, etc.

Administrative corruption

Administrative corruption as a form of corruption refers the implementation of existing laws, regulations, and decrees. The role that political and upper level administrative corruption have come to play in contributing to the profound and enduring malaise for societies, States and firms alike. Administrative corruption for example, spreads if corrupt officials have to pay an entry fee and have to resort to other citizens to finance the entry fee, allowing to additional groups of voters to have a stake in corruption. Combating administrative corruption has been approached by reforming public administration and public finance management.

Political influence

A new type of corruption, referred as uninstitionalized political influence was directly generated from the rise of new groups of wealth and power during modernization and their efforts to make themselves effective in politics in a political system that was slow to provide legitimate channels. The modernization theory on corruption derived in the hypothesis to sustain that the more rapidly a country modernizes, the higher the level of corruption. The process of modernization in developing countries contributed to generate high levels of corruption through the expansion of governmental activities, the rise of a new rich social class seeking political influence and change of social values and.

Political influence allows private individuals to help shape public law and depends on the size of the firm and interactions with state officials, rather than direct payments. The judiciary, legislative and executive systems may be weak to political influence. Political influences can buy the decisions of the legislative, executive and judiciary actors even in a party system. Victims of a corrupted legislative, judiciary or executive systems lacking of political influence make illicit offerings to gain access to public goods, government jobs and resources. Political influence of the higher-rank officials can be modeled as a function of their revenues from collecting relatives. There are some models to capture large political influences such as the lobbying models and the probabilistic voting models which analyses contributions of small group voters.

State capture

State capture is defined by the World Bank as the actions of individuals, groups, or firms, both in the public and private sectors, to influence the formation of laws, regulations, decrees, and other government policies to their own advantage as a result of the illicit and non-transparent provision of private benefits to public officials. State capture as a form of corruption surrounds the formation of laws, regulations, and policies. One form of state capture is decision altering which encompasses bribes and promises of bribes to alter or affect decisions, affect policy formulation and formation of laws, regulations, or decrees in order to benefit the bribing person or entity. State capture is also a phenomenon of undue influence and capture of the State by powerful firms. The extent, level and degree of State capture and monopolistic vested interests vary significantly across countries. Firms engaged in illicit influence experienced higher growth rates than firms that did not engage in this form of corruption. Where state capture is a major constraint for multinational and domestic firms as a whole, they suffer by growing more slowly while the firms that are purchasing laws and regulations obtain higher benefits and growth faster and higher.

Generally, state capture cannot be abolished by democratic institutions. State capture has been associated with corruption and lobbying literature with campaign expenditures which are linked to policy outcomes. State capture and administrative corruption are identified as significant issues to be confronted by transitional economies. The character of corruption matters with respect to the functioning of the political, economic and administrative system. Corruption in different forms and areas, state capture and distrust are mutually reinforcing and may be prevalent to differing degrees depending on the specific State. Countries in economic transition with high levels of both forms of corruption, administrative and state capture are associated with output decline, poverty, inequality, and even organized criminal activity. This report recognizes that the state capture poses formidable challenges, status quo often benefits powerful interests and the political economy of anticorruption initiatives has proven complex and difficult. The institutional vacuum in countries with transitional economies provided ideal opportunities for state capture.

Typology of Cahn and Gambino (2008)

Cahn and Gambino have developed a corruption typology based on natural resources, commodity dependence, and good governance in different contexts identifying four broad categories of countries in Sub-Saharan Africa. This typology is intended to emphasize the importance of poor governance to underdevelopment and clarifies the need for different strategies for countries in four different categories.

Category 0 denotes the near-absence of both effective governance and significant levels of foreign investment. Higher levels of corruption.

Category 1 denotes countries highly dependent on a single-source of export revenue and economic dependence that creates opportunities for corruption and can have antidemocratic consequences.

Category 2 includes countries that have a broader range of export commodities characterized by substantial levels of external investment and governments that are more interested in decreasing corruption and improving the business environment.

Category 3 includes nations where country governance is much improved and vastly better than other countries, economies are diversified, with strong agricultural sectors, and levels of foreign investment are reasonably high. Lower levels of corruption.

Corruption typology of Merat and Roth Deubel (2008)

Merat and Roth Deubel use the typology of both formal and informal institutions which distinguishes informal institutions according to the complementary, substitutive, accommodative and competitive types. Merat and Roth Deubel analyze on the basis of North's neoinstitutionalist framework violence and corruption corresponding with the presence of informal institutions and powerful armed groups who compete with the formal institutions and pursue divergent goals, drawing from the case of the municipality of Tumaco, Colombia. In this case, the local institutional level, where the balance of power is in favor of informal institutions, is the most affected.

Corruption typology of Pedersen and Johannsen (2008)

The typology used by Pedersen and Johannsen (2008) for measuring corruption distinguishes:

Day-to-day corruption that takes place at the lower levels of the administrative hierarchy related to ways of behavior that are necessary and appropriate to get things done and administrative malpractice.

Grand corruption is at the middle and higher level of public administration and directly in the political sphere that circumvents legitimate democratic decisions and decision making. This type of corruption is related to the specific context of transforming and redefining private-public relations in society.

Pedersen and Johannsen (2008) illustrate how this typology may be applied in terms of concrete position in the political and administrative sphere, in the following table.

Table 3: Identification of the 'provider' of corruption

Grand corruption	Parliament
Grand corruption/ Administrative malpractice	Ministers
Administrative malpractice	Top level officials
	Intermediate level officials
'day-to-day' corruption	Lower level officials

Pedersen and Johannsen (2008)

Corruption typology of Transparency International (TI) UK

Based on economic and political defense analysis, the Transparency International UK has developed a typology of corruption as a framework for defense. In one of the main categories of the typology of defense corruption, political context and control, corruption in the defense establishment under democratic political authority encompasses, over-elaborate and non-agreed defense policy, hidden defense budgets, underestimated or off-budget defense spending, cronyism and dishonest leadership level, secret power networks, organized crime links, misuse and control of intelligence for corrupt purposes, misuse of investigatory powers, misuse of power to influence legislation and parliamentary investigations, corruption of the judicial process, involvement in elections and politics, and ultimately state capture, de facto illicit takeover of defense by officials.

Table 4: Corruption – framework for defense

Political Context and Control	Defense Processes	Defense Personnel
Defense policy	Procurement, bribery, diversion of funds	Values, standards, rules, weak, ignored.
Defense budgets, not transparent, debated or audited	Salaries, diversion of funds	
Leadership and accountability, dishonest, unclear or split	Property and sales	Small bribes
Organized crime links	Personal control of secret budgets	Money for security
Control of intelligence	Private businesses	
State capture	Reward, promotion, disciplinary, failures, inequities	Job preferences

Source: TI UK (2009)

One set of problems with the literature on corruption typology is that it offers a very narrow definition of corruption, whereas there is a need to proffer one comprehensive framework for analyzing a wider typology of corruption phenomena.

Levels of corruption

Corruption is present on both the low and high levels of the bureaucracy and also both types of corruption are linked by corruption on the intermediate levels of the bureaucracy. Levels of corruption indicate where corruption can be encountered.

Alemann (1995) has proposed the following levels of corruption:

Vertical levels of corruption

- local politics (micro level)
- middle level, regions (meso level)
- nation-state level (macro level)
- international level (mega level)

Horizontal areas of corruption

- administration of housing and construction
- agencies of economic development
- procurement administration
- licenses, approvals
- military procurement
- secret services

A well know characterization of levels of corruption considers individual, business and political corruption.

Individual corruption takes place primarily in relations between individual citizens and public officials and authorities.

Business corruption takes place primarily in relations between enterprises/companies and public officials and authorities.

Political corruption takes place in the higher echelons of public administration and on a political level.

Levels of corruption are associated with economic and political factors although it is hard to establish a robust causal link between levels of corruption and levels of economic performance. The same is truth for a relationship between levels of corruption and levels of political development.

According to the modernization hypothesis, the modernization process brings corruption. Countries with faster developing economies tend to have higher levels of corruption. Therefore, Countries that modernize faster tend to have higher levels of corruption that could be perceived as the result of "the law of inertia" by which parts of the society pioneer in modernization while other parts were reluctant to change. However, some developing countries challenge systemic corruption and have lower levels of corruption than some wealthy countries.

Functionalists emphasize the positive effects of corruption on development arguing that corruption is likely to increase the efficiency of government, overcome bureaucratic obstacles and divisions in ruling elite that might otherwise result in destructive conflict. These arguments are rejected by empirical research. They also show that high levels of corruption are associated with lower levels of investment and economic growth.

Some economists agree that there are significant correlations between high levels of corruption and economic consequences such as the inefficiencies in the operation of markets, distorting the composition of public expenditure by focusing spending on activities likely to yield large bribes and reducing the level of direct foreign investment by adding costs and creating uncertainty. Large government spending is associated with lower levels of corruption. More decentralized countries have lower levels of corruption. Countries that have relatively low levels of corruption may attract significantly more investment than those perceived to be more prone to corrupt or illicit activity. Higher levels of corruption are associated with greater government intervention in economy. The public choice theory asserted that large government sectors are associated with higher levels of corruption. Firms can contribute to have higher levels of corruption by seeking rent compete for government contracts and licenses not through price mechanisms but through bribes to public officials.

States with high levels of corruption are not incompatible with high levels of economic growth although if those states had been able to reduce their levels of corruption, they would have experienced even higher rates of economic growth. In a large robust dynamic economy, the economic costs of low levels of corruption are minimal, while in a fragile, unbalanced, stagnant economy, the economic costs of high levels of corruption are insupportable. Countries that tolerate relatively high levels of corruption are unlikely to perform high rates of economic growth although may enjoy still decent rates. High levels of corruption may tend to increase imports of goods and services. In developing economies there seems to be significant correlation between high levels of corruption and lower levels of investment and growth. Based on cross-country perceived corruption studies finds a direct link between high levels of corruption and low levels of foreign direct investment and that corruption is strongly negatively associated with the investment rate. Corrupt procurement practices reduce growth by reducing the productivity of public investment, increasing public investment that is not adequately supported by nonwage expenditure on operation and maintenance, reducing the quality of the existing infrastructure and by decreasing the government revenue needed to finance productive spending.

An institutional factor that matters for corruption is the fairness of the legal system, not the efficiency of the legal system. In policy strangling regulation leads to higher levels of corruption. The relationship between corruption and trust in informal institutions makes the most effective means to obtain goods and services, which in turn increases the levels of corruption. Mistrust creates an inefficient public sector that in turn raises levels of corruption and undermines popular trust in the state. Thus, corruption and the lack of institutional trust feed each other, producing a vicious circle. Social groups may contribute to higher levels of corruption by seizing the opportunity to exploit the power vacuum and expanding the groups' interests at the expense of the society. Countries with higher levels of human development have lower perceived levels of corruption, as measured by the control of corruption index. Higher levels of corruption are correlated with lower school enrolment and higher dropout and illiteracy rates, blocking key routes out of poverty. Countries with high levels of corruption also have higher levels of poverty. Inequality leads to low out-group trust, which in turn leads to high level of corruption. Land reform and the initial adoption of industrial policy produced different levels of inequality, and thereby different levels of corruption and social trust. Countries with low levels of corruption tend to have fewer conflicts and can exacerbate the impact of natural disasters.

3.   THEORETICAL PERSPECTIVES

The state is central to any analysis of corruption in Africa. Indeed, there is virtually no subject that one considers in Africa without emphasizing the role of the state. This is so because the state not only leads, it also embodies the society in Africa. One fundamental fact to note from the onset is that the Nigerian state, like most African states and Third World countries is a product of colonialism. It is not surprising therefore that many theorists of African politics trace the problem of political corruption to the debauchery of colonial rule. Among the theories of African politics that has helped in the understanding of Africa's predicaments, and more importantly the issue of endemic corruption, include theory of two publics developed by Peter Eke, Prebendalism popularized by Richard Joseph and Gurnal Myrdal's soft state thesis. Others have captured Africa as a rentier, Patrimonial and Neo-patrimonial state. These theories are credible not only in the understanding of the state and its predicaments in the African countries but also in providing important explanations for the pandemic corruption ravaging African countries. For instance, Ekeh argued that one of the most striking impacts of colonialism was the emergence of two public realms, the primordial and civic public realms which, related differently with the private realm in terms of morality.

For Nigeria, and generally for Africa, Ekeh has argued; only rights (i.e. benefits) are expected from the state by its citizens, who owe duties (responsibilities) to a native sector. The former forms the basis of an "amoral civic public realm", and the latter a "moral primordial public realm". Therefore, the civic public realm was associated with illegitimate and exploitative colonial rule and had no moral linkages with the private realm. It was an amoral public realm in which cheating the system was considered a patriotic duty. The result is that as the same actors operate in the two realms, the state apparatus is employed to fatten the nest of the primordial public, thereby making corruption, nepotism and ethnicity to mention a few the hallmark of the civic public. A good citizen of the primordial public gives out and asks for nothing in return; a lucky citizen of the civic public gains from the civic but enjoys escaping giving anything in return whenever he can. But such a lucky man would not be a good man were he to channel all his lucky gains to his private purse. He will only continue to be a good man if he channels part of the largesse from the civic public to the primordial public. That is the logic of the dialectics. The unwritten law of the dialectics is that it is legitimate to rob the civic public in order to strengthen the primordial public. The 'acme of the dialectics', according to Ekeh is corruption which takes two dimensions- the embezzlement of public fund from the civic public and the solicitation and acceptance of bribes from individuals seeking services provided by the civic public by those who administer these services.

Though Ekeh's thesis has provided for some time, a sound framework for understanding the impact of colonialism on Africa, and the explanatory framework for the endemic corruption ravaging the continent, it is important to note that the robbery in the civic public was not, neither is it currently employed to strengthen the primordial public but rather further pauperize it. In fact, the primordial sentiment is nothing but an instrument of political deception, trickery and manipulation in the hands of the privileged political and bureaucratic elite for personal aggrandizement and less for group benefits. With the benefit of hindsight, most of the stolen state wealth has been siphoned abroad by the political class to acquire estates in developed countries, buy chieftaincy titles across the country and establish a "political empire". Though some of the ill-gotten wealth may trickle down to the primordial public in this process, as Ekeh also documented, it is undoubtedly insignificant to strengthen it, more particularly if strengthening in this sense is construed in terms of social, economic and political development. The parlous state of development in African states and communities is a testimony to this fact. High level of illiteracy and crippling poverty; the prevalence of preventable diseases and so on are evidences that the primordial public is at the receiving end of all corrupt practices. Ironically, the primordial public provides a safe haven for the milito-bureaucratic and political elite who are obsessed to stealing public funds. Thus, these milito-bureaucratic and political elite now constitute a socio-political cult, gang or group with distinct character in Nigeria.

The politico- bureaucratic public has elitist character which have "unlimited" access to the state wealth. They are found in every sector and among all the ethnic groups constituting the Nigerian state and are monolithic in outlook. The ideology and philosophy of these political gangsters can be simply stated thus- wherever you see the state wealth, steal it. They are bonded and cemented by common atrocities and fierce contest in the bid to outsmart one another in the pilfering business, generate conflicts and instability in the society. As powerful as they are, they constitute a fragment of the society with both local and international connections. Right from independence, political power has been oscillating among these group and their anointed children. This they strive to protect and further consolidate by politicizing ethnicity and religious identity. The fact that they constitute a cult in Nigerian politics is incontestable. Few scholars are likely to dispute Richard Joseph's linking of corruption and the fall of the Nigerian Second Republic to the prebendalisation of state power. In what seem to be a re-characterization of Ekeh's theory, Joseph contends that "The politics of competition over allocation of resources, or what in Nigeria is called 'the national cake', has its most dire consequences the transformation of the offices of the state into prebends…"

According to the theory of prebendalism, state offices are regarded as prebends that can be appropriated by office holders, who use them to generate material benefits for themselves and their constituents and kin groups. While clientelism and prebendalism might be mutually reinforcing, these concepts have separate meanings. Clientelism defines the nature of individual and group relationships within the broader social and political space, but prebendalism are essentially a function of the competition for, and appropriation of the offices of the state (Seteolu 2005). "Clientelism assists to understand the mechanism of (how) class control legitimizes the lopsided distribution of resources among social groups and enhances the status of the political elite" (Seteolu 2005:36).

30

Therefore, Nigerian political culture is hinged on clientelism and prebendal politics which further enhance our understanding of the prevalence of political corruption. The pursuit of politics is intended to appropriate the political space and resources among fractions of the political elite. The Nigerian state also has a patrimonial and neo-patrimonial character. Patrimonialism means that the distinctions between the public and the private domains have become blurred and power, which has become a major source of wealth, has become personalized. Within this framework of analysis, the behaviour of political elite in Africa is linked to traditional value system. The African society is patriarchal where political power is personalized, and leadership is permanent in the context of self-recruited.

According to Seteolu, these socially imbibed values are replicated in the political terrain where contending coalitions accumulate resources to offset side payments required to retain or expand followership in the context of power politics. The fierce struggle in the public space is linked to conflicts that characterize leadership succession in traditional political systems and the attractions of political control where party politics guarantee access to wealth and economic power. Therefore, the political elite use social identities such as ethnicity for particularistic purpose. The ethnic identity becomes a mobilizing mechanism to access political power, consolidate dominance and economic control. Consequently, it is not impossible for power to be used for personal or group aggrandizements. In patrimonial societies, corruption seems to be intrinsically part and parcel of the political culture. Neopatrimonialism, a related term to prebendalism and new form of patrimonialism is a term used to describe and explain state failures in Africa. It is used to describe patrons using state resources in order to secure the loyalty of clients in the general population, and is indicative of informal patron-client relationships that can reach from the very high up in state structures down to individuals in the lower levels (like in the small villages). As a result of that kind of patron-client or identity politics, Nigeria has regularly been one of the lowest ranked nations for political transparency by Transparency International (TI) in its corruption perception Index. With such politicization of primordial rivalries, the political class and opportunistic bureaucrats found a safe sanctuary to embezzle and squander state resources. The problem of corruption therefore, is inextricably tied to the problem of identity and the problem of citizenship. It is rooted in the psycho-political perception of Nigeria by an average Nigerian.

The problem is also rooted in history. For example in 1947, Obafemi Awolowo one of the foremost nationalists wrote, Nigeria is not a nation. It is a mere geographical expression. There are no "Nigerians" in the sense as there are "English", "Welsh", or "French". The word "Nigerian" is merely a distinctive appellation to distinguish those who live within the boundaries of Nigeria from those who do not. In 1948 Sir Abubakar Tafawa Balewa a leader of the Northern Peoples Congress was quoted as having said that, Since 1914 the British Government has been trying to make Nigeria into one country, but the Nigerian people themselves are historically different in their backgrounds, in their religious beliefs and customs and do not show themselves any sign of willingness to unite. Nigerian unity is only a British intention for the country. Thus, while a Nigerian nationality is non-existent properly speaking citizenship is operative at the homeland level. The existence of the legal cum political conception of citizenship in Nigeria is queasy. In his words, beyond phrase-mongering, there are no citizens in Nigeria, only citizens of Nigeria. That is, Nigerian citizenship is merely geographical, it is without moral-ideological content... part of what typifies citizenship, especially in the modern state, is the de-emphasising of geography and other natural facts in its composition... the freedom to locate anywhere within the boundaries of the relevant geo-polity is nonexistent in Nigeria. Undoubtedly, there is absence of genuine citizenship sentiment at the national level. Hence the struggle and agitation for political representation by the various ethnic groups are meant to secure access to the common wealth.

Therefore, the idea of federal character principle entrenched in section 14 sub-sections 3 and 4 of the 1999 constitution and the idea of rotational or zoning arrangements (popular among the political parties), besides ensuring sense of national belonging and the promotion of national unity, has embedded corrupt tendencies. The fact is that it is not genuinely invoked. It was designed not only to settle group conflicts over the distribution of resources or promote a sense of belonging to the nation but primarily to create access to the state wealth by the few privileged elite who see the state wealth as belonging to none. In one word, zoning formula and federal character principle are elitist in form and content. In Nigeria today, the success of an ethnic group or a politician is synonymous with the level of access of such group to state resources, defined in term of the number of political appointments such group is able to secure in the political arrangement. This to a large extent also, in the common erroneous thinking in Nigeria, determines the group percentage share of the national cake. Therefore, to steal from the common wealth is an acceptable norm. It was a misconception that this is used to fatten the primordial public. Contrarily, it has only been used to further fatten the purse of the politico-bureaucratic elite at the peril of the primordial public. The privileged elite have successfully disillusioned the psyche of the masses with the virus of ethnicity, even to the extent that when corrupt acts are unveiled and the perpetrator(s) are under probe, it is customary in Nigeria to associate such probe with ethnic politics. And question such as – How many Hausa, Ibo or Yoruba are under probe or how many have been punished are not uncommon. The question would not be how many Yoruba/Hausas/Ibos as the case may be are involved in corrupt acts. Virtually anything in Nigeria can be ethnicized. This perhaps explains why corruption has remained endemic despite all efforts to curtail it. Consequently, sanctioning offenders have become problematic.

Thus, Gurnal Myrdal soft state thesis becomes very apt in Nigeria. In Gurnal Myrdal's soft state thesis, propounded in the light of the Asian experience, we come to grips with the paradox of the post-colonial state and its predicaments, most especially as it relates to the problem of corruption. A soft state whether democratic or undemocratic is bedeviled with the inability to institute reforms or enforce social discipline. It is a state where the legal system and its paraphernalia are moribund or at least ineffective. Even when framing policies, the authorities (under the control of politico-bureaucratic elite) are reluctant to place obligations on the people, especially in matters of corruption. A soft state, is one in which formal rules (laws, officially stated administrative rules and practices, etc.) are applied copiously and in a lax manner rather than vigorously and consistently...it is one in which private advantage can be gained and private bargains struck concerning the enforcement or non-enforcement of the rules, as when a businessman bribes a tax official...Besides money, another inducement is kinship sentiment and another is the favour of superiors Therefore, one of the damaging consequences of the politics of identity is that it tends to render the state soft. Laws are discriminately applied and the anti-corruption laws are not an exception. Therefore, one of the characters of a soft state is its over-permissiveness of corruption and corrupt acts. In conclusion, it is not improper to x-ray corruption in Nigeria through the prisms of prebendalism, clientelism, patrimonialism, neopatrimonialism, soft state thesis and the theory of two publics. However, the point of departure is the argument that robbery and the profligacy in the public sector have further pauperized the primordial public rather than fattening it. The stolen wealth circulates among the milito-bureaucratic and political elite irrespective of their regional, religious or ethnic identities. The consequence of which is preposterous and counterproductive.

4.   CAUSES OF CORRUPTION

Corruption is a phenomenon that takes place due to the presence of a number of factors. An understanding of such factors requires, among other things, a kind of general framework for a clearer understanding of the causes of corruption, especially from a broader perspective. Genesis of corruption can be explained by looking at three levels-international, national and individual institutional levels. Competitiveness of international markets provides multinational companies of various sizes with an incentive to offer bribes to gain an advantage over competitors. At the national level basic development strategy of any government moulds opportunities and incentives for corruption. At the same level three relationships - between the government and the civil service, between the government and the judiciary and between the government and the civil society-also affect the nature and discussions of corruption. Three areas of government activity-customs administration, business regulation and management of foreign aid - act as sources of corruption at the level of individual institutions. Corruption also results from the presence of a number of factors. These include: rapid economic and social change, strong kinship and ethnic ties, new institutions, overlapping and sometimes conflicting views about what is proper public behaviour, governmental monopoly over economic activities, political softness, widespread
poverty and socio-economic inequalities, ignorance, lack of knowledge about individual entitlements, communal bonds, ambivalence towards legitimacy of governmental organizations, asymmetric relationship favouring those in control of state power, economic shortages in which public officials assume extraordinary control over scarce goods and services, greed, patronage and systematic maladministration.

Most of the above-mentioned factors contributing to corruption can be categorized into 'six-fold typology'. This typology contains ideological, external, economic, political, socio-cultural and technological variables. Some of the major reasons as to why people "collude in different ways, rationalize corrupt practices and tolerate corruption in a large scale" are because of the presence of number of factors. These are: governments act as monopolies in many respects, discretion that government and its monopolistic public agencies enjoy in their decision making and allocative roles, lack of effective accountability in government except in the nominal sense of presenting annual audited accounts and reports to parliament or answering questions in the parliament, citizens have limited information about the rules of the game and the standards of service they can expect from public agencies, and exposure of the average citizen to corruption in the public sector tends to be episodic.

History and Culture

Various theorists—as well as many popular accounts—attribute countries' different rates of corruption to particular historical and cultural traditions. A surprising range of national cultures, spanning all continents, have been thought conducive. According to Guy Wint: In nearly all Asian countries there has always been a tradition of corruption. Public office meant perquisites. Russian writers from Karamzin to Gogol have claimed distinction for their country. According to Prince Bakunin, "There is stealing and corruption everywhere… but in Russia I think there is more stealing and corruption than in any other state". Within Western Europe, southern Italy is the home of 'amoral familism'-including the propensity to offer and accept bribes—and Spain is home to amiguismo, the "use of contacts and intermediaries in dealings with the bureaucracy, and influence trafficking in political life". Further west, the Argentine playwright Mario Diament asserts that: "corruption in Latin America is not merely a social deviation, it is a way of life and one historian has written of a "culture of corruption" in colonial Spanish America. Other scholars argue, more broadly, that a culture of distrust and private-spiritedness fosters higher rates of venality than occur in communities where generalized trust and civic engagement are strong. Distrust and suspicion boost the demand for corrupt services on the part of private agents. The greater perceived uncertainty of entering into partnerships with strangers may impede legitimate private business activity. This may render transactions with family members and close acquaintances-including corrupt exchanges with friends in public office-relatively more attractive. The suspicion that competitors are getting ahead through corrupt acts and that regulatory officials will impose predatory sanctions if not paid off may make a business strategy of keeping one's hands clean seem counterproductive. At the same time, the lack of trust and civic engagement may increase the supply of corrupt services by reducing the danger to officials of being exposed and punished. Societal organizations to monitor and protest abuses will be weaker.

A related argument links corruption to ethnic polarization. In deeply divided societies, the demand for corrupt services may be higher at any given price. For one thing, generalized trust is likely to be lower. Members of ethnic groups may feel that demanding favors from co-ethnics in office is the only effective way to obtain government services. At the same time, the supply of corrupt services may be increased by the social leverage that ethnic leaders have over officials of their ethnicity: fear of social ostracism may make them reluctant to refuse their co-ethnics' demands. Various scholars have argued that competition between different ethnic groups within the same state has at times fostered patronage politics and bureaucratic predation. Easterly and Levine find a relationship between ethnic fragmentation and growth-retarding public policies.

Economic Development

Both the demand for and the supply of corrupt services may be greater in less developed societies. Social mores regarding corruption are often thought to vary with the level of economic development. In "traditional" societies, such transactions may not be clearly stigmatized, reducing the danger for those on both sides of the corrupt exchange. Public and private spheres tend to be less sharply delineated. According to Gunnar Myrdal, in underdeveloped countries "a bribe to a person holding a public position is not clearly differentiated from the 'gifts,' tributes, and other burdens sanctioned in traditional, pre-capitalist society or the special obligations attached to a favor given at any social level." When giving presents to officials can be defended as accepted etiquette, businessmen are likely to have fewer scruples about seeking favors in return.

Others have viewed corruption not as a characteristic of underdeveloped societies but as a consequence of their rapid modernization. Abuses of public office for private gain become prevalent as new sources of wealth and power seek influence in the political sphere at a time when the regulatory authority of the state is expanding and social norms are in flux. Rising economic elites are likely to bid with money for greater political access and privilege, using their wealth to open doors into the decision-making organs of the state. At the same time, modernization disrupts the political institutions and weakens the social norms that might have restrained officials from selling their authority.

Political Institutions

Various conjectures link the supply of corrupt services to characteristics of countries' political systems and state structure. Democracy is sometimes thought to increase the cost to officials of corrupt transactions, reducing the supply. The institutions of a free society—free press, secondary associations, etc.—may make exposure more likely, as may the practice of electoral politics. Particular legal systems may also offer private businesses greater protections from predatory officials. La Porta et al. have argued that the nature of a country's legal traditions-common law vs. French-style civil law-influences the quality of state protection and enforcement of private property rights. Such legal traditions may also affect the supply of corruption. In a fairly crude sense, the size of the state may influence the supply of corrupt public services. Some have suggested a simple positive relationship between state size and corruption or rent-seeking. The greater the share of GDP redistributed by government, the greater the spoils for corrupt allocation. Similarly, the more officials there are in public office, the more potential bribees available. However, the potential cost to office-holders of exposure will depend on the internal rules and ethos of the bureaucracy. The more meritocratic is recruitment and the greater the extent to which bureaucracies offer predictable and rewarding long term careers, the greater may be a bureaucracy's internal discipline and the greater the incentive for staff to avoid possible dismissal.

Industrial organization arguments suggest that the internal structure of the state may also influence the supply of corrupt services. When bureaucracies are more decentralized, with less internal discipline, bureaucrats may compete to extract maximal rents.

In more decentralized or federal states, the burden of corruption may thus be greater. According to James Q. Wilson, one cause of corruption in the US system is "the need to exchange favors to overcome decentralized authority". Another political scientist argues that

"decentralized political systems are more corruptible, because the potential corrupter needs to influence only a segment of the government, and because in a fragmented system there are fewer centralized forces and agencies to enforce honesty." A number of economists have also suggested that corruption will be more widespread at the local level, perhaps because of the greater intimacy and frequency of interactions between private individuals and local. According to Heywood, in Spain "the creation of new regional administrations during the 1980s offered extensive opportunities for the development of a new spoils system, operated by the party in power".

On the other hand, some have argued that competition between subjurisdictions with greater autonomy may reduce corruption and the checks and balances of a federal system may limit the center's ability to conceal malfeasance. Susan Rose-Ackerman suggests that a federal structure in which each level has its own police force can reduce the vulnerability of any one law enforcement agency". The danger that additional levels of regulatory authority in the state may lead to a greater total burden of regulation and corruption may thus be offset by the beneficial consequences of competition between jurisdictions at lower levels. Political systems differ not just in the nature of political institutions or governing regimes but also in how often these change. Two arguments trace differences in the supply of corruption to the degree of political instability—with opposite implications. Some authors argue that by shortening the time horizons of those in power, political instability inclines them to make money fast and crudely rather than to moderate their current appetites for the sake of future earnings.

Wars, civil wars, revolutions, and other occasions on which legal and social order is weakened are often times of rampant abuse of power. Prevailing disorder may also reduce the danger of being detected and punished.

Others have suggested an opposite conjecture: too much stability enables officials to reach long-term, relatively secure corrupt bargains with private partners. Wars, invasions, major political change, and turnovers of government may actually sweep away the debris of accumulated deals. Some commentators saw in the longevity of the Japanese LDP and Italian Christian Democrats an explanation for the corruption scandals that weakened them in the 1990s. Britain, which has avoided invasion and occupation since 1066, experienced a flowering of corruption in the 18th Century. More recently, Barbara Geddes has argued that when a new party comes to power it will have greater incentives to reform the corrupt practices of its. By contrast, political institutions that support continuity and avoid political alternation may increase corruption. According to David Hine, "the existence of broad forms of consociational power-sharing (whether at national level, or between different tiers of government)" features among the causes of political corruption in contemporary Europe.

Public Policies

Finally, some argue that whatever the nature of political institutions, it is the policies actually adopted by those in power that determine the extent of corruption. In economies with extensive state regulation, greater opportunities for venality exist. The supply of rents for officials to allocate will be higher than in more liberal settings. Economies that are open to foreign competition will see such rents eroded, reducing the value of restrictions on domestic production. According to Ades and Di Tella, countries that are more open to foreign trade tend to be less corrupt. Third, to the extent that exposure means (at least) dismissal and the loss of future earnings, higher civil service wages may reduce the relative attraction of venality to officials, reducing the supply of corrupt services.

Other causes are:

- The false perception of government as "they" as opposed to "us" thereby making the people detached from the government. And so, their business is to get as much as from the government as they can without getting into trouble.

- Lust for power: The struggle by individuals and groups to get position of authority at all cost induces corruption. This usually manifest in bribes, electoral malfeasance.

- Legitimacy Crisis: In Nigeria today, most of the political office-holders assumed power through fraudulent means, which is undemocratic and illegitimate in a democracy. Such leaders tend to suffer identity and legitimacy crisis. And one of their strategies to garner popular support is the free distribution of public funds to influential people who could help them achieve peoples' support.

- Paying to get a government benefit: The government buys and sells goods and services, distribute subsidies, organizes privatization of state firms, and provides concessions. Officials frequently have a monopoly of valuable information. These activities create incentives and urge for corruption. When the government is a buyer or a contractor, there are several reasons to pay off officials. First, a firm may pay to be included in the list of qualified bidders. Second, it may pay to have officials' structure bidding specifications so that the corrupt firm is the only qualified supplier. Third, a firm may pay to be selected as the winning contractor. Finally, once a firm has been selected, it may pay to get inflated prices or to skimp on quality.

- Paying for official positions: When corruption is pervasive, positions in the state bureaucracy become valuable assets, and there will be derived demand for jobs in the state sector. In developing countries there is a lively market for positions in the bureaucracy that generate large bribes.

- Delay and Red Tapism: Some officials delay unnecessarily so as to induce payoffs. This can happen either in contracting and auctioning or in administering regulatory and tax laws.

5.   INCIDENCE OF CORRUPTION IN NIGERIA

According to the report released on December 3, 2014, Nigeria scored 27 out of out of a maximum 100 marks to clinch 136th position out of the 175 countries surveyed. This means that Nigeria has 'improved' by eight points against its 2013 rating as 144th out of 175 countries. A statement issued from the Berlin office of Transparency International shows that more than twothirds or over 75 percent of the 175 countries surveyed this year scored below 50, on a scale from 0. Countries within the 0-50 range are perceived to be strikingly corrupt (New Telegraph Editorial, 2014). The table below equally captures Nigeria's rating by Transparency International between 1996 and 2014.

Table 5: Nigeria's Corruption Perception Index Rankings, 1996-2014

Year	CPI Score out of 100%	Rankings
1996	6.9	54 out of 54
1997	17.6	52 out of 52
1998	19	81 out of 85
1999	16	98 out of 99
2000	12	90 out of 90
2001	10	90 out of 91
2002	16	101 out of 102
2003	14	132 out of 133
2004	16	144 out of 145
2005	19	152 out of 159
2006	22	142 out of 163
2007	22	147 out of 179
2008	27	121 out of 180
2009	25	130 out of 150
2010	24	134 out of 178
2011	24	143 out of 183
2012	27	139 out of 176
2013	25	144 out of 177
2014	27	136 out of 174

Put together, a few things stand out in the report regarding corruption in Nigeria. First, the document indicates that the tag of corruption in Nigeria is quite high, while public perception of government's crusade against graft suggests that it may be nothing more than a façade. This view is reinforced essentially by the perceived kid gloves with which both government and anticorruption agencies like the Economic and Financial Crimes Commission (EFCC), the Independent and Corrupt Practices and Other Offences Commission (ICPC) and the Code of Conduct Bureau (CCB) treat corruption related offences. There are also allegations that these agencies are selective in their prosecution of corruption cases. We do not have many cases of diligent prosecution of corrupt persons. Corruption cases are hardly ever pursued to a logical conclusion. There are so many inconclusive cases, and many instances of corruption that the agencies declined to prosecute. In many of these glaring cases, successive governments in the country have failed to convince anyone that Nigeria is committed to checking graft.

Nigeria was ranked the 35th most corrupt country in the world by the Transparency International (TI) in 2012. In 2013, Nigeria moved by two steps to clinch the position of the 33rd most corrupt country in the working, according to TI. The level of corruption in Nigeria has eaten deep into the fabric of the Nigerian society and that has been responsible for the crises of development in the country. Another way of stealing in Nigeria is through the self-increment of salaries by the members of the National Assembly without recourse to the constitutional body that is responsible for fixing the salaries of elected public officers. According to Awojobi, "the lawmakers have perfected a system of increasing their own salaries, which make them earn more than their foreign counterparts."

The annual basic salaries of Nigerian lawmakers and their counterparts in some rich nations are displayed below:

Table 6: Annual basic salaries of Nigeria and some advanced countries

Countries	Basic Salary
Nigeria	$189.500
United States	$174.000
Canada	$154.000
Japan	$149.700
Germany	$115.500

Source: Ameh & Oladimeji (2014)

Nigeria has close to 170 million people. Well over 100 million Nigerians live in destitution, the third country in the world with a large number of poor (World Bank). The irony of this is that Nigeria with a very low standard of living, the federal lawmakers earn more than lawmakers of countries mentioned above with a good standard of living. According to Nigerian Professor Ibrahim Gambari, the Special Adviser on the International Compact with Iraq and Other Issues for the Secretary-General of the United Nations in 2008, berated the Nigerian lawmakers for their dishonest ways of increasing their salaries which according to him affect the provision of good roads, railway system, power supply and capital projects. The high level of political corruption and its aftermath effect on the nation's development prompted the Obasanjo government to establish the Economic and Financial Crime Commission (EFCC) in 2004. Mohammed (2013) gave a summary of details of political corruption cases be handled by the EFCC.

Table 7: EFCC Corruption Cases

S/N	Name	Case Status	Amount Involved	Status Suspect(s)
1	Ayo Fayose (former Governor of Ekiti State)	Arraigned on 51 counts	N1.2 billion	Case pending, granted bail
2	Adenike, Grange (former Minister of Health)	Arraigned on 56 counts	N300 million	Discharged and acquitted
3	Joshua Dariye (former Governor Plateau state)	Arraigned on 23 counts	N700 million	Case pending, Granted bail since 2007
4	Saminu Turaki (former Governor Jigawa state)	Arraigned on 32 counts	N36 billion	Case pending, Granted bail since 2007
5	Oji Uzor Kalu (former Governor Abia state)	Arraigned on 107 state counts	N5 billion	Case pending, Granted bail since 2008
6	James Ibori (former Governor Delta state)	Arraigned on 170 counts	N9.2 billion	Case pending, Granted bail since 2008
7	Iyabo Obasanjo (former Senator)	Arraigned on 56 state counts	N10 million	Case pending, Granted bail since 2008
8	LuckyIgbinedion (former Governor of Edo state)	Arraigned on 191 state counts	N4.3 billion	Case determined, ordered to pay $25 million as fine
9	Gabriel Aduku (former Minister of Health)	Arraigned on 56 state counts	N300 million	Discharged and acquitted
10	Jolly Nyame (former Governor of Taraba	Arraigned on 41 state counts	N1.3 billion	Case pending, Granted bail since

11	Chimaroke Nnamani (former Governor of Enugu state)	Arraigned on 105 state counts	N5.3 billion	Case pending, Granted bail since 2007
12	Michael Botmang (former Governor of Plateau state)	Arraigned on 31 state counts	N1.5 billion	Case pending, Granted bail since 2008
13	Roland Iyayi (former MD of FAAN)	Arraigned on 11 state counts	N5.6 billion	Case pending, Granted bail since 2008
14	Prof. Babalola Borishade (former Minister of Aviation)	Arraigned on 11 state counts	N5.6 billion	Case pending, Granted bail since 2008
15	Boni Haruna (former Governor of Adamawa state)	Arraigned on 28 state counts	N254 million	Case pending, Granted bail by court since 2008
16	Femi Fanikayode (former Governor of Adamawa state)	Arraigned on 47 state counts	N250 million	Case pending, Granted bail since 2008
17	Bode George (PDP Chieftain)	Arraigned on 68 state counts	N100 billion	Jailed in October 2009
18	Rasheed Ladoja (former Governor of Oyo state)	Arraigned on 33 state counts	N6 billion	Case pending, Granted bail since 2008
19	Senator Nichola Ugbane; Hon. Elumelu and others	Arraigned on 158 state counts	N5.2 billion	Case pending, Granted bail since 2009
20	Hamman Bello Hammed (Ex CG Customs)	Arraigned on 46 state counts	N2.5 billion	Case pending, Granted bail since 2009
21	Adamu Abdullahi (former Governor of Nasarawa state)	Arraigned on 149 count charge	N15 billion	Case pending, Suspect on court bail
22	Attahiru Bafarawa (former Governor of Sokoto state)	Arraigned on 47 count charge	N15 billion	Case pending, Granted bail by court
23	Hassan Lawal (former Minister of Works)	Arraigned on 37 count charge	N75 billion	Case pending, Granted bail by court
24	Kenny Martins (Police Equipment Fund)	28 count charge	N7,740 billion	Case pending, Granted bail since 2008
25	Esai Dangabar, Atiku Abubakar Kigo, Ahmed Inuwa Wada, John Yakubu Yusufu, Mrs. Veronica Ulonma Onyegbula and Sani Habila Zira	16 count charge	N32.8 billion	Case pending, Granted bail by court

Source: Mohammed 2013

These are high profile corruption cases that involved huge sums of money, most of the accused persons are past governors and ministers of the federal republic of Nigeria. If this massive amount would have been channelled for the provision of amenities in the country, Nigeria would not have the problems of erratic power supply, bad roads, poor health services, insecurity, high rate of poverty, high level of unemployment and the high rate of dropout of school-aged children.

In another development, corruption has been blamed for the insurgency that is threatening the co-existence of Nigeria has a nation, notable personalities such as Noble laureate, Professor Wole Soyinka and the former United States President Bill Clinton have said that political corruption is responsible for the high level of insecurity being experienced in the northern part of Nigeria. In a similar same vein, the United State Under Secretary for State for Civilian Security, Democracy and Human Right, Sarah Sewall has stressed that corruption is the main obstacle to the fight against the insurgency group, Boko Haram, according to her, "despite Nigeria's $5.4 billion security budget for 2014, corruption prevent supplies as basic as bullets and transport vehicles from reaching the front lines of the struggle against Boko Haram" (Ameh and Oladimeji, 2014).

The military has come out to say lack of weaponry stall their fight against Boko Haram, which prompted the federal government to make a proposal to the National Assembly for the approval of $1 billion for the procurement of military hardware. The question that was asked by the renowned Human Rights lawyer and Senior Advocate of Nigeria (SAN) Femi Falana, what has happened to the budgetary allocations to the Defense Ministry in the past. Just as Nigerians are still debating the issue of the $1 billion, the South African government impounded a private jet from Nigeria that is owned by one of the popular pastor in Nigeria, Ayo Oresejafor with $9.3 million. The Nigerian government said the money was meant for the purchase of arms to fight Boko Haram, but the South African government sees the confiscated money as an act of money laundering. If the Nigerian government claimed the money was meant for arms, why did the government not follow due process to buy arms from overseas instead of stuffing $9.3 million on a private jet with two Nigerians and an Israeli? The Lagos State governor, Babatunde Fashola, stresses that the $9.3 million confiscated by the South African authority has made Nigeria a laughing stock globally. On his part, with reference to the seized $9.3 million, the former Archbishop of Lagos, Anthony Cardinal Olubunmi Okojie posit that:

Corruption is in every nation but Nigeria's own is number one. I am telling you. And if we are not careful, this nation will go down the drain. Now, people can't help you to bring something from that corner without asking for remuneration. Look at so many children and youths who have no school to go to, or no money to pay school fees, and there are rich men who parade themselves up and down the place as rich people. For what? They seem to have forgotten that this life is not the end. Nobody chose his parents, and nobody came into the world with a gold or silver spoon. The $9.3 million can build hospitals, roads, schools, supply water, drugs and restore some of the capital infrastructures that have been dead for a while.

6.   COSTS AND CONSEQUENCES OF CORRUPTION IN NIGERIA

Albeit unscientific, the above represents an effort to catalogue the brazen and outlandish plunder of Nigeria's resources that could have been devoted to development. The worst part of all this is that the thieving elites do not invest the booty in their own country, to build factories and railroads-as did America's "robber barons" in the nineteenth century. Rather, Nigeria's kleptocrats spent the booty lavishly on mistresses, luxurious automobiles, fabulous mansions -- on consumption, not productive ventures. The rest of the loot was spirited out of the country into foreign bank accounts to develop the already advanced countries-a double whammy.

Bribery, embezzlement and theft-sometimes on a grand scale-divert enormous resources from public coffers into private hands. Unchecked, it eventually blossoms into a "culture of corruption." Nigeria is a typical case where corruption has mushroomed and spilled over on to the international scene with various "advance fee" frauds and scams. This pattern of looting has become so deeply ingrained that it is difficult to eradicate.

Inefficiency

Corruption has several deleterious effects on economic development. First, it breeds inefficiency and waste. Contractors and suppliers fail to deliver because they have bribed some official. Who you are and how big a kickback you offer matters more than how well or efficiently you perform a job. As a result, contracts are inflated and some kickbacks paid to some conniving official. Work done is shoddy: Roads are poorly constructed and wash away at the first drop of rain. Telephones refuse to work, postal service is non-existent and the entire communication system is in shambles, costing the country billions in lost output.

Infrastructure has crumbled in Nigeria because contractors failed to perform. The educational system has sharply deteriorated. Roads are pot-holed. Hospitals lack basic supplies because they have been stolen or diverted, and patients are often asked to bring their own bandages and blankets. State institutions decay and break-down. Nobody cares because tenure of office and promotions are based not on competence and merit but on personal loyalty to the president, ethnicity, and sycophancy. Institutions such as the civil service, the judiciary, parliament, and the police disintegrate and fail to function since they have all been perverted.

The rot is not confined to one area but seeps into all areas of government. Parliament becomes a joke; a rubber stamp. The police, the military and the civil service-all are hopeless. Even though the state soaks up scarce resources (through heavy taxation), it fails to fulfill its role in facilitating economic growth or deliver essential services. Nigeria has many fine lawyers, but the judiciary is tainted by trials settled with bribes. It has fine academics, but universities are tarnished by the trade in diplomas. It has respected chiefs, but the nobility has been mocked by the sale of chieftaincy titles. In many ways, the institution which has suffered the most under this military regime is the military itself. Military men are not soldiers anymore is a common Nigerian observation. Nigerian cities have fire departments, but often there is no equipment.

Institutional break-down and the failure to provide the most basic essential services creates an environment inimical to development. The cost of doing business in such an environment increases enormously. Simple, routine applications takes weeks to be approved. Security of persons and property can seldom be guaranteed. Increasing production becomes chancy, given intermittent disruptions in the supply of electricity and water.

Soaring Government Deficit

Second, corruption aggravates the budget deficit problem. Expenditure figures are padded. Ghost workers proliferate on government payrolls. An audit task force appointed by the Nigerian Government said on 1 November 1996 that it had discovered 28,000 'ghost workers' on the state payroll. The 'ghost workers' are either fake, retired or dead persons whose names remain on the payroll for fraudulent officials to claim their wages. Revenue collectors are notoriously corrupt, pocketing part of tax proceeds, waiving taxes if they receive large enough bribes. Deters Foreign Investment Third, corruption drives away foreign investors: Government contracts in Nigeria, say international businessmen, are among the most expensive in the world 'mainly because of excessive margins built into such contracts for personal interests.' Those personal interests can be seen attending expensive schools in Britain, or parked outside plush government villas: a Maserati or Lamborghini is quite normal for an army chief. Africa has remained a wilderness to foreign investors for a variety of reasons: weak currencies (except notably in extractive industries, where output is priced in dollars), exchange controls, a feeble local private sector, poor infrastructure, small domestic markets, stifling bureaucracy, political instability, uncertain legal system, and corruption. Despite fanciful ads, elaborate investment codes, and guarantees of profit repatriation, Africa attracts less than 5 percent of the direct investment going to the developing countries, an estimated $2.5 billion or so in 1994. In 1995 when a record $231 billion in foreign investment flowed into the Third World, Africa's share fell to a miserly 2.4 percent.

Crumbling infrastructure, chronic instability and corruption have deterred foreign investors. Even French investors are shying away from Africa. Africa's share of French overseas investment dwindled from $500 million in 1983 to $170 million in 1992, Jean-Pierre Ranchon [vice president of the Council of French Investors in Africa] said. Asia's grew from $4 million to $600 million over the same period. But why should foreign investors be excoriated when Africa's kleptocrats do not invest their own wealth in their own countries? Asked Herman Cohen, former U.S. Assistant Secretary of State for African Affairs in 1991: "Over the last 10 years, Africans themselves have exported $20 billion a year into bank accounts in Europe [and the U.S.] buying real estate. So if Africans don't have confidence in their own continent, why should the rest of the world?

Economic Contraction and Collapse

Fourth, corruption leads to economic contraction and collapse. Corruption and capital flight, which flourish under non-democratic systems, seriously stunt economic development. At an April 2000 press conference in London, U.N. Secretary-General Kofi Annan lamented that: Billions of dollars of public funds continue to be stashed away by some African leaders – even while roads are crumbling, health systems have failed, schoolchildren have neither books nor desks nor teachers, and phones do not work. While corruption and capital flight exist under all political systems, their incidence tends to be more pervasive when rulers are not held democratically accountable. Africa's experience shows that a corrupt government is incapable of efficient economic management and eliciting the sacrifices necessary for the development effort. A corrupt African government cannot attract foreign investment or spur domestic investment. Like the colonial state, the predatory African state is also extractive. Under colonialism, Africa's resources and wealth were plundered for the development of metropolitan European countries. Today the tiny, parasitic ruling elites use their governing authority to exploit and extract resources from the productive members of the society. These resources are then spent lavishly by the elites on themselves or siphoned out of Africa.

Popular Rebellion and Social Upheaval

By far, however, the most serious has been the severe damage rampant corruption has wrought on the international reputation of Nigeria and the self-image of its people. The name "Nigeria" itself is now synonymous with scam or fraud. Over the years, Nigeria's governments have steadily lost credibility with the people. People became alienated and no longer trusted their government. They saw the state, not as a "partner in development" but as enemies to be evaded, cheated and defeated. In the Niger Delta, are in open rebellion against the government. Nigeria's oil wealth is produced in the Niger delta, which has been the scene of increasingly violent rebellion. Nigeria's state oil company, working with partners that include Shell, Chevron, Mobil, Amoco and Texaco, produces 2.4 million barrels of oil- worth $30 million to $40 million-each day. But for years, most of that river of cash has flowed to military governments that have broken promises to spend fixed percentages of it to bring electricity, clean water, village clinics, and schools to the oil belt. The regime of General Sani Abacha, for example, promised to return 13 percent of Nigeria's oil proceeds to develop the oil communities but the funds were siphoned off by corrupt officials. "If we would honestly put even 3 percent of the oil revenues into these communities, it would make a big difference", said Frank Efeduma, a Shell oil spokesman in Warri, Nigeria. In the 1990s, the Ogonis, Nembe, Ijaws and other ethnic groups escalated protest to violence, often seizing oil facilities and oil company workers.

The entire delta area with 6 million people, consisting of 20 tribes, has been devastated. As The Washington Post put it: "The curse of natural wealth has fallen heavily around the Niger River delta, Africa's most lucrative oil field. Nearly 40 years of oil production, directed mostly by military governments, has left the delta peoples poorer, sicker, less nourished and less educated than the rest of the country. Oil spills have damaged fishing grounds and farmland" . For instance, in Nembe, home to several thousand people on the edge of Nigeria's largest oil field, there is no electricity, clean water, or roads or other basic amenities. Gas is burned there, causing environmental pollution. Nor does the area have a major oil refinery. In a policy that defies economic sense, oil is piped from the delta area hundreds of miles to the north, where it is refined to provide employment and industrial activity to the Hausa-Fulani, who have monopolized political power since Nigeria's independence in 1960.

Hardest hit in the Niger delta are the Ogoni, who number 500,000 and sit on top of billions of dollars of oil reserves. But "we get no benefit from it, absolutely none", complained Chief Edward Kobani, a senior elder of the Ogoni. Their homeland is an environmental mess. Gas-a by-product of the oil industry for which there is no use — is burned 24 hours a day, producing acid rain and toxic pollution. Air and water quality has suffered, and crops damaged. The health toll is enormous: There are high levels of skin rashes, allergies, abscesses and infections. Ken Saro-Wiwa started the Movement for the Survival of the Ogoni People (MOSOP), demanded $10 billion for environmental damage and royalties from the federal government and Royal Dutch/Shell, and threatened to secede the area from Nigeria. The group wrote an Ogoni national anthem, designed a national flag, and printed a national currency. Frightened of another Biafra, the military government attacked Ogoni villages. In May 1995 Saro-Wiwa was arrested; he and eight others were hanged on November 10, 1995 despite a chorus of international pleas for clemency. But the Ogoni have not given up their fight; nor have others in the Delta region.

The delta youths demand not just equity from the state but also in the redistribution of income from their oil. A first attempt at secession was led by Isaac Adaka Boro, who called for a Niger Delta Republic in 1965. The rebellion was short-lived and faded into history, but the anger in the delta was reignited with Saro-Wiwa's MOSOP. The Abacha military regime, as well as western oil companies, felt threatened. Despite Saro-Wiwa's hanging and the militarization of the entire Ogoniland, the groups were not deterred.   On October 4, 1998, militant Ijaws seized oil facilities throughout their land. At the Batan station, they ordered the pumping station's crew to shut it down and leave. "We are like mad dogs", said Augustine Egbane, an Ijaw leader. The oil field at Batan was producing 26,000 barrels-worth $380,000-a day but little money went back to the village.

In the 35 years that Shell operated the Batan field, oil spills have spoiled the village's traditional livelihood of fishing. Further, villagers must paddle for three hours to find clean water. The village has no clinic and no real school, only an unequipped classroom that villagers built themselves. In 1993, a government development agency strung electrical lines in the village but never connected them to the outside.   Fast-forward to present day realities, there has not been any meaningful changes in the status-quo, if any at all, it is an intensification of violence with different groups springing up such as Niger Delta Avengers who have taken it upon themselves to blow up strategic pipeline installations thereby affecting oil production output which has made Nigeria fallen behind Angola as the highest oil producing black Nation.

Corruption is linked to the development of organized crime, including the involvement of criminal syndicates in money laundering and trafficking in people and drugs. In Colombia, for example, narcotics trafficking is the source of much of the country's corruption at high levels. Alliances exist between politicians and the illegal armed groups that make money off of a lucrative trade in cocaine, and want to see their business continue.

Grand corruption

When one considers the economic consequences of corruption, the adverse impact of grand corruption comes readily to mind. Corruption on a grand scale associated with some dictators and their cronies can involve embezzlement of huge sums of public funds, and the mismanagement, wastage, inequity, and social decay that come along with it, can be disastrous for an economy. There are familiar tales of fortunes in gold, gems and jewelry stashed away in secret hiding places by corrupt officials and hundreds of millions of dollars spent in acquiring real estate abroad and in depositing into their foreign bank accounts. The devastating impact of misconduct on such a massive scale, especially for poor countries that are facing perennial and severe foreign exchange shortages, is obvious and requires no further comment. But corruption does not have to be on a grand scale to inflict serious damage. There are other adverse effects that can be just as damaging for a poor country. These deserve a closer look and are taken up below:

Rise of the underground economy – Underground economic activities exist in all countries. They are of two types. First, there are those that are illegal such as engaging in the drug trade or the smuggling business. The second consists of those activities that are legal but are not officially recorded to evade taxes or for some other reason. Corruption gives rise to both these types of activities and contributes directly to the rise of the underground economy. Although underground economic activities exist in all countries, they become pervasive where corruption is widespread. When a large portion of an economy goes underground, official macroeconomic data which mostly cover only the formal sector, become unreliable to assess economic performance or to provide a basis for policy making and analysis. Official foreign trade statistics, for example, no longer reflect a country's true volume, or value, of exports and imports because of large illegal and unrecorded movements of goods and services across the border in a thriving smuggling business.

Similarly, the official exchange rate becomes symbolic and generally meaningless when foreign exchange dealings are mostly transacted in the parallel market and at the unofficial exchange rate which bears no relation to the official rate. The inflation rate, based on the consumer price index (CPI), also becomes suspect as the consumer basket of goods and services which is used to calculate CPI, may not adequately cover items that consumers have to purchase in the unofficial market at exorbitant prices. Likewise, the official interest rate – a continuing source of dismay, frustration and headache for the formal banking community – may not reflect the true cost of capital and may diverge considerably from the more realistic interest rate at which a large volume of financial transactions takes place in the informal credit market. Similar problems arise with respect to other key macroeconomic indicators. Under these circumstances, proper economic accounting and macroeconomic management become difficult. In the absence of reliable data, transparent policies, and proper macroeconomic management, there is not much hope for economic development, modernization, or emergence of a well-functioning market economy.

Income distribution

Under a corrupt system, the privileged and the well-connected enjoy economic rent. Economic rent, by definition, represents abnormal or monopoly profits and can bestow large benefits. As such, there is a tendency for wealth to be concentrated in the hands of a tiny minority of the population. Income distribution, therefore, becomes highly uneven. In addition, the burden of corruption falls more heavily on the poor as they cannot afford to pay the required bribes to send their children to a decent school, to obtain proper health care, or to have adequate access to government provided services such as domestic water supply, electricity, sanitation and community waste disposal facilities. An undesirable situation can arise as in some countries where through illegal connections to the water mains, the water sprinkler system in a golf course operates most of the day to keep the grass green on the fairways, while villagers living across the street do not have sufficient water for their daily household needs. At night, through payment of bribes, the driving range of the golf course is ablaze with floodlights, while children in the nearby village have to do their homework by candlelight in support of the government's energy conservation effort.

Consumption pattern

Closely associated with an unequal income distribution and concentration of wealth in the hands of a few, there emerges a distorted consumption pattern aimed at meeting the lifestyle of the new and extremely rich urban elite. This involves import of a large variety of luxury goods from abroad – flashy cars, lavish home furnishings, state-of-the-art consumer durables and electronic products, fashion clothing, exotic perfumes, expensive foodstuffs, fine wines and spirits, and fancy goods of all kinds that can be found in supermarkets and department stores of any prosperous Asian city in the heyday of the region's economic boom. Most of these goods are, of course, beyond the reach of ordinary citizens in the cities and in the countryside. Conspicuous consumption with expensive cars cruising along dirt roads, and conspicuous construction with luxury apartment buildings rising amidst poverty and squalor, bring home the point that affluence is not widely shared in these countries.

Impact on investment

Corruption's adverse impact on private investment, both domestic and foreign, is considered to be particularly harmful for a developing economy. Bribes may have to be given before any investment takes place and upon entering into negotiations for the establishment of an enterprise. More payments usually follow in the process of setting up the business. Procurement of leases for land and buildings; permission to engage in activities such as production, transport, storage, marketing, distribution, import and export; obtaining connections for water, gas, electricity, and telephone; having access to telex, fax and e-mail facilities and so on; can involve payment of substantial bribes at various stages and may require the services of agents with specialized expertise on how to get around complex rules and procedures to acquire these things. Unfortunately, these agents and middlemen, instead of being part of the solution can often become a part of the problem.

Their services do not come cheaply and they add to the cost and complexity of doing business under a corrupt regime. Then, when the enterprise is finally established and up and running, corrupt officials may demand cuts from the firm's earnings. Moreover, in order to establish and maintain good public relations, and for continued viability of the enterprise as a business concern, entrepreneurs may have to contribute to all sorts of charities and worthy causes that are unrelated to their line of work. Bribe payments constitute a form of tax on enterprises. But they represent a pernicious type of tax as bribery deals have to be struck in a surreptitious way and bribe-givers cannot always be certain that bribe-takers will live up to their part of the bargain.

It is also a regressive form of tax. Its burden falls more heavily on small businesses in trade and service sectors as these small entrepreneurs normally do not enjoy political patronage. Hence, corruption not only raises the initial costs of investment but by substantially increasing risks and uncertainty for a venture, can significantly reduce the incentive to invest.

For a poor country, talented local business people, managers, entrepreneurs, and industrialists represent a scarce and valuable resource. Their talents should not be wasted in rent seeking activities. They should be doing productive work. For them to invest and engage in productive work will require not only political stability but economic stability as well as a measure of predictability and honesty on the part of the government. Surveys have also revealed that business people have to spend a lot of management time in discussions, negotiations and waiting for appointments with bureaucrats and public officials in corrupt regimes than in countries where there is less corruption. As for foreign direct investment (FDI), the benefits it can bring to a developing country are well known. FDI helps augment the much needed capital resources in a poor country. What is more important, it can also bring technology, knowhow and managerial and marketing skills that improve a country's international competitiveness, help develop valuable market outlets abroad, and strengthen foreign contacts and broaden the outlook of its business community.

Moreover, foreign investment can increase employment opportunities, assist in improving labour skills, and can produce useful goods and services for the domestic market. It can also be crucial in building modern infrastructural facilities, establishing reliable energy generating and distributing systems, setting up high technology communication networks, providing efficient transport links with the rest of the world and in developing capital markets and business and financial services which are essential for a country to become a modern, developed nation. In short, FDI can play an important role in assisting a country to modernize and to more fully develop its productive potential.

The above advantages of FDI will be forthcoming to a country only if it provides a conducive climate for foreign investment. FDI will not come in a big way where policies are unclear and inconsistent, relevant and reliable economic information and data to plan and make sound business decisions are hard to come by, and the courses of action and measures the government is likely to pursue on the major issues facing the economy are difficult to fathom and to predict.

Long term investment decisions cannot be taken under such conditions. Both the quantity as well as quality of foreign capital inflows into the country will therefore be adversely affected. The type of investment that foreigners would be willing to undertake in this uncertain economic climate would mostly consist of activities to exploit the country's natural resources or to engage in quick yielding ventures that have little beneficial spread effects and backward and forward linkages with the domestic economy. Investments in setting up facilities to assemble, package and label imported parts and components for export represent a good example. These activities bring little in the way of local value added, or in imparting skills and technology to help a poor country in its industrialization effort. At a more fundamental level, corruption makes it difficult for a low income country to establish and maintain domestic and internationally acceptable "rules of the game" which are necessary for orderly and proper conduct of investment and business activities. This deficiency is believed to be an important reason why the least developed countries in the world are poor. It is also believed to be a reason why some of them will remain that way.

Effect on the government budget

Corruption can have undesirable consequences on both the revenue and expenditure sides of the government budget. The consequences on the revenue side are more familiar. Paying bribes to reduce taxes, fees, dues, custom duties and public utility charges such as for water and electricity, are common in many countries. Bribes are also used to make illegal water, electricity, gas and telephone connections to have access to these facilities without paying for the services obtained. All these result in serious losses of revenue for the government. Fraud, embezzlement and misappropriation of public funds add to the losses. The consequences on the expenditure side are more insidious.

Corruption adversely affects the composition of government expenditure. This is because large benefits can be realized from corrupt deals on expenditure items that are expensive, whose costs are not readily apparent, and which are considered to serve some high national priority concern so that they have to be undertaken in a discreet and secretive way. Purchase of jet fighter aircraft, for example, ideally meets these requirements. This item is costly, it is not something that one can buy in a supermarket and find out its price, and it is required to safeguard national security – a high national objective which no one wants to compromise or to appear unpatriotic by questioning its usefulness.

Moreover, acquisition of fighter jets is politically sensitive and hence the deal has to be handled with considerable discretion. Large and expensive projects whose costs are hard to determine but with huge potential for kickbacks and economic rent are also good candidates for corrupt deals and hence for inclusion in the national budget. On the other hand, not much money can be made by spending on teachers' salaries, in buying school textbooks, or on projects on rural preventive health care or training programmes to meet a shortage of a vital labour skill in industry. Corrupt regimes therefore tend to devote a large share of their national budget expenditures on acquiring sophisticated military hardware and on large projects, and less on education and health, and on other priority needs that would contribute towards overcoming critical bottlenecks in the economy and help ease hardships that most ordinary people face in their daily lives.

Social costs

In any society, there are laws and regulations to serve social objectives and to protect the public interest, such as building codes, environmental controls, traffic laws and prudential banking regulations. Violating these laws for economic gain through corrupt means can cause serious social harm. There are many instances of this throughout the Asia and Pacific region. For example, there have been numerous cases where soil erosion, resulting from illegal logging, has led to whole villages being washed down hill sides in flash floods or buried in mud slides, taking a heavy toll in lives. Violating building codes through the connivance of corrupt officials and building contractors has resulted in collapse of apartment buildings, department stores and hotels in some countries.

Failure to observe proper fire prevention and safety regulations has caused supermarkets, hotels and discos, filled with shoppers and customers to go up in flames. Overloaded ferries and passenger ships have sunk in seas and rivers all over the region. Paying bribes to operate un-roadworthy and poorly maintained public vehicles have led to accidents on the highways and buses plunging down ravines and gorges due to mechanical failure are common in many countries. There has also been growing concern over corruption in large infrastructure projects such as dams and bridges.

A huge project, estimated to cost over $7 billion is a source of particular worry. Shoddy workmanship, use of substandard materials and disregard for proper design and engineering specifications, due mainly to corruption, have caused bridges to collapse and dams to burst, resulting in heavy loss of life and property. Obscure insider trading practices and financial scams that can result from poorly supervised financial systems also have serious economic and social consequences. People have lost their life savings and fortunes in financial scams. This has led to massive street demonstrations and civil unrest in several east European countries. Lack of transparency, shady deals and corrupt practices have also been a contributing factor to the financial and macroeconomic crisis that has swept across East and South-East Asia.

Price controls, subsidized goods and black markets
It is a common practice in many developing countries to institute price controls and to provide essential goods and services at subsidized prices to consumers. The official price for a key food item, such as rice, is fixed by paying a low administratively set price to farmers, while gasoline, electricity and charges for public transport and other essential items are provided at low subsidized prices. These mostly benefit city dwellers as they are the main consumers of these subsidized goods and services. The urban bias in the provision of subsidized food and other necessities stems from the political reality that city dwellers, especially the large masses at the lower end of the income scale, are more

politically conscious, better organized and are easier to be instigated into civil unrest than the rural poor. It is usually discontent in the cities that ignites social and political upheavals in a country.

Fixing prices at artificially low levels lead to demand exceeding supply for the subsidized goods so that the all too familiar shortages, rationing, corruption and black markets result. Several undesirable consequences follow. First, there is a loss of potential government revenue. For example, when those that have access to subsidized gasoline, such as government officials and car owners, sell it on the black market at several times the official price, they make large profits. These profits could be expropriated as revenue by the government, if there is no subsidy, no price distortion, and gasoline is valued at its true opportunity cost, that is, charged by the government at its market clearing price. Second, setting low farm prices on rice and other agricultural products, to provide cheap food for city dwellers, means farmers are subsidizing the people in the cities.

Likewise, low prices set on gasoline and energy contribute to deficits in the government budget. When these deficits are met out of the general budget, is tantamount to the rest of the country, and especially the rural sector, subsidizing the consumption of these goods and services by the urban sector. Third, fixing low prices on rice and agricultural products, in the wake of sharp increases in the prices of other domestically produced and imported goods (such as fertilizers), turns the terms of trade against farmers. This adversely affects their incentive to produce and hence agricultural output. Fourth, low prices set on energy result in huge losses for the government enterprises engaged in this area.

Consequently, they do not have the resources to invest in new facilities, to buy spare parts or to properly maintain existing machinery and equipment that are falling into disrepair. Some machines and transmission lines that are still in use may have outlived their useful economic life. The outcome is frequent breakdowns, unreliable and poor service, and general inability to meet requirements in terms both of generating capacity and in the quality of energy produced. Finally, under-pricing energy has other detrimental effects. Cheap energy leads to its uneconomic and wasteful use. Moreover, when energy prices are kept at a level much below cost for decades, there is little incentive for its users to adopt energy efficient technologies and methods of production. So they are not sufficiently prepared for the large price adjustment that inevitably comes when low prices are no longer sustainable due to an internal or an external shock.

The result is disruption in production, more corruption as bribery will be resorted to in order to avoid payment of the higher charges, and increased inflationary pressures as higher energy costs will be passed on to consumers by raising prices. Thus, price controls, subsidies and the corruption and black markets they generate, can lead to undesirable social and economic consequences. This also illustrates the point that dismantling controls, getting rid of subsidies, preventing price distortions, and "getting prices right" in general, form a key element in economic reforms and for the establishment of a properly functioning market economy.

Impact on economic reforms

Unfortunately, corruption places severe constraints on a country's capacity to undertake economic reforms. This is because reforms require greater transparency, accountability, free and fair competition, deregulation, and reliance on market forces and private initiative, as well as limiting discretionary powers, special privileges, and price distortions – all of which will reduce opportunities for economic rent on which corruption thrives. The rich and the powerful, the main gainers of a corrupt system, will therefore oppose reforms.

7.   **CORRUPTION AND UNDERDEVELOPMENT INTERFACE: THE CASE OF NIGERIA**

Corruption, Poverty, Inequality and Unemployment

Corruption is a canker worm that has reduced development in all sectors of the economy. Corruption has been the primary reason behind the country difficulties in developing fast. This is the reason why transparency international has consisted rating of Nigeria as one of the top three most corrupt countries in the world. In Nigeria, the level of corruption, level of poverty, unemployment, inequality, poor state of our electricity, transport sector, health sector, education sector and communications is the major problem of economic growth and it is a major handicap for doing business in the country. For sure, the issue of poverty is not a new phenomenon in Nigeria. Almost all previous regimes have contended with the issue. By mid-1999, for example, when the country returned to democratic rule, the percentage of people who were considered to be below the poverty line (leaving on less than $1USD per day) was estimated to be as high as 70% (Sela-i-martin and Subramanian, 2008). In recent times, however, the problem is receiving more serious attention of policy makers in Nigeria. This point was brought home following the devastating youth militancy in Nigeria's oil producing Niger Delta region and more recently the violent insurgency in the impoverished North Eastern region where a radical Islamic sect, known as Boko Haram, has decreed a Muslim caliphate killing at least 13000 in the process. Most Nigerians will easily blame the high rate of poverty in the country for these conflicts.

The major indicators of poverty, according to the World Bank, are: lack of freedom of action and choice; lack of adequate food, shelter, education and health; vulnerabilities to ill health; economic dislocation; maltreatment by public agencies; and exclusion from key decision-making processes and resources in society. Poverty, it was noted, "is the result of economic, political, and social processes that interact with each other and frequently reinforce each other in ways that exacerbate the deprivation in which people live. Although the Nigerian government has often disputed the claim that poverty is

66

increasing in the country, and what constitute the actual poverty rate in Nigeria today remains a subject of considerable debate among development agencies and scholars, most statistics show that, indeed, poverty levels in Nigeria is unacceptably high. For instance, official data published by Nigeria's National Bureau of Statistics shows that percentage of Nigerians living in abject poverty, calculated on $1 USD per day, based on an adjusted purchasing power parity, had increased from 54.7% in 2004 to 61.2 % in 2010 (National Bureau of Statistics, 2012).

A recent report by the World bank figures suggests that poverty rates in Nigeria are significantly lower than estimates based on the 2009/2010 NBS study. In the Banks view, per capita poverty rate registers at 35.2 and 33.1 percent of the population in 2009/2010 and 2012/2013, respectively (World Bank, 2014:17). This is still very high considering that Nigeria is a huge country. According to the World Bank, Nigeria with 7% of the world's poor people now ranks as the third largest contributor to the worlds poverty figures, next to China (13%) and India (32%) (Ogunbiyi, 2014). Poverty levels also vary widely across the country's geo-political zones. The proportions of the population in these zones that were 'food poor' in 2010 were: North-Central (38.1%); North-East (51.5%); North-West (51.8%); South-East (41.0%); South-South (35.5%); and South-West (25.4%).

The contradiction of rising poverty in a rapidly expanding economy has made Nigerian commentators to support the general hypothesis that corruption leads to poverty, or at least contributes to it substantially. According to this hypothesis, corruption manifests in many forms of waste and misallocation of resources by government officials which denies the down-trodden of vital social services and infrastructures, indirectly fueling poverty.

There are two major contending definitional perspectives on poverty. The first definitional perspective defines poverty basically in terms of income, which could be defined in several ways. One of such ways is to define it as a percentage of people living on an income of less than $1 or 2 USD per person per day, usually in terms of purchasing power parity (PPP). Another way could be to calculate poverty as corresponding to the lowest income quintile in a referenced population. The first approach is however a more preferred one. But even that itself has many critics who argue that measuring poverty in terms of income will not fully capture the phenomenon (Chetwynd, 2003:6). According to this perspective, a broader definition which conceives poverty not as a one dimensional issue but as a multidimensional phenomenon covering income, food intake, education, health, security, etc., will be more useful. As Chetwynd argues, measuring poverty in terms of income level is relatively straightforward, while the multi-dimensional approach is more complex and involves factors that are difficult to quantify. However, this problem has been solved more or less by the UNDP Human Poverty Index, which measures poverty in terms of life expectancy, education and economic indices.

Table 8: Incidence of Poverty in Nigeria

Year	Poverty Incidence (%)	Estimated Total Population (in Millions)	Population in Poverty (in Millions)
1980	28.1	65	18.26
1985	46.3	75	34.73
1992	42.7	91.5	39.07
1996	65.6	102.3	67.11
2004	54.7	126.3	69.09
2010	69.0	163.0	112.47

Source: National Bureau of Statistics, 2007: 5; 2012

Table 9: Relative Poverty by Sector - Urban and Rural (%)

Year	Urban	Rural
1980	16.2	28.3
1985	37.8	51.4
1992	37.5	46.0
1996	58.2	69.3
2004	43.1	63.8
2010	61.8	73.2

Sources: National Bureau of Statistics (2007: 36; 2010)

Table 10. Trends in Poverty by Geo-Political Zone (%)

Zone	1980	1985	1992	1996	2004	2010
South-South	12.2	45.7	51.1	58.2	51.3	37.6
South-East	12.9	30.4	41.0	52.5	34.1	34.3
South-West	12.4	38.6	42.1	60.9	43.2	42.0
North-Central	32.2	50.8	46.0	64.7	63.4	62.3
North-East	35.6	54.9	54.0	70.1	67.6	63.0
North-West	37.7	52.1	36.5	77.2	63.9	62.9

Source: National Bureau of Statistics (2007: 38; 2012)

In recent times also, no institution or sector of our nation has been spared of corruption including, religious bodies, educational institutions, judiciary, military, MDAs, the private sector, and all the rest. Instances of corrupt practices have been extensively reported in the local media. Others can be found in reports of dozens of official inquiries established by governments at all levels. Many academic studies have also been done. Further, over the last 10-15 years Nigeria's anti-corruption agencies have also investigated and successfully prosecuted several corruption cases shedding further light on the nature of corruption in contemporary Nigeria. Thus Nigerians have much reason to worry about the level of corruption and its effect on their society. Yet, contrary to widespread perception, not all of these forms of corruption have contributed to the poverty situation in Nigeria. For example, petty corruption, such as the extortion of petit sums by police men may have several implications for law and order, or legitimacy of government, but is hardly linked to the material situations of the poor in Nigeria. On the other hand, many other forms of corruption, especially grand corruption involving the diversion of hundreds of millions or even billions of dollars of public funds, can perpetuate poverty in many ways.

There are several;

One example is the diversion of funds meant for poverty alleviation programs such as foreign aid, which reduces the amount of resources available for poverty eradication programmes. Although, in theory some of these resources could still be spent on other areas not related to poverty alleviation, even if they were not stolen. It is however more likely that a greater percentage will be available to serve the purpose for which they were intended. Corrupt practices of this type will then discourage donors from giving further aid. Nigeria is known to be among the least recipients of foreign aid, not only because donors perceive the country as relatively endowed, but its history of corruption also serves as a disincentive. Even if the country does not receive foreign aid, grand corruption may also affect the government's own poverty eradication programmes. For instance, Government own funds or procured items for poverty alleviation can be misappropriated. The commonest example being fertilizers usually procured for small scale farmers but end up being diverted by government officials. This leaves the poor rural farmers poor even where their conditions could have been improved (Liverpool-Tasie, 2010:12).

Another example is where grand corruption or the embezzlement or diversion of huge public funds leaves the population with poor infrastructure or none at all, further deepening their poverty. Examples of such infrastructure include health and educational facilities, and of course roads. In Nigeria, contracts are usually awarded for many of such projects, but in some cases, the projects will be abandoned after the contractors have collected huge amount of money, sometimes up to 100 per cent of contract sum. In 2007 the Human Right Watch published report on such type of corruption in Rivers state, one of Nigeria's leading oil producing states and geographic heart of Nigeria's booming oil industry. The report detailed the misuse of public funds by local officials in many of the state's local governments, and their harmful effects on primary education and basic health care. For instance the report observed that in five local governments researched by Human Rights Watch in Rivers, local administrations have failed to make more than nominal investments into health care and education. Much of the money that could have gone into improving these services has been squandered or outright stolen. Human Rights Watch found that one local government chairman habitually deposited his government's money into his own private bank account. Another has siphoned off money by allocating it towards a "football academy" that he has not built. According to state and federal government officials, civil society activists and other sources, these problems mirror the situation in most of Rivers' local governments. (HRW, 2007).

Also in early 2007, a top grandee of the ruling PDP and former boss of Niger Delta Development Commission, NDDC (Onyema Ugochukwu), an interventionist agency created to address the problems of poor infrastructure and low standard of living in Nigeria's oil producing region, was arrested and arraigned before an Abuja High Court by the Economic and financial Crimes Commission, EFCC an anti-corruption agency accused of embezzling and diverting billions of naira. This was made possible by deliberately inflating several road construction contracts intended for some of the impoverished oil producing communities. Sadly, some of the diverted funds were lost having been deposited in a local Societe Generale Bank which later succumbed to distress.

One can also cite some examples in the energy sector also. In early 2012, probes by federal legislatures revealed massive fraud and corruption in the lifting of crude oil and importation of refined petroleum products by licensed private operators, commonly referred to as oil marketers, or the Oil Cabal. These fraud were usually perpetrated with the active connivance of government officials (Kalu, 2012). One of the consequences of these crimes have being that, in recent years, Nigerians, have grappled with the challenges of artificial scarcity and high cost of petroleum products, especially Kerosine, which is widely used by the poor. Similar problems have been experienced with electricity supply. In June 2012, a parliamentary probe of some recent power projects found that over $16 billion USD had been spent between 1999 and 2007 without any visible improvement in the nation's electricity supply (The Guardian, June 30, 2012). At its peak, the combined electricity generation capacity stands at about 4000 megawatts. As a result, more than half of the country's 167 million inhabitants have no access to electricity, while the rest have to rely on expensive generators, run on diesel supplies controlled by a small and powerful cartel of importers (Reuters, 13 February 2012). Not only is electricity available to a small proportion of the population, it is also erratic in supply: up to 40 % of Nigerian firms" costs come from running power generators to cover for electricity shortages (Anaro, 2012). What this means is that most of the poor are shut-out from electricity to power their homes and more importantly their business which helps worsen their poverty.

Some types of grand corruption could also leave a large segment of the population without any form of social security/safety net. A few examples will suffice here. In January 2012, a top official of the Nigerian Police Pension Fund (John yakubu Yusuf) was convicted by an Abuja High court for embezzling N2 billion in one of the largest pension fund scam ever discovered in the country. His action will undoubtedly mean several retired officers will not get their pension plunging them into a life of penury post-retirement (The Nation, January 12, 2012). Corrupt practices perpetrated by private sector actors may also have similar impact. In the early 1990s, most Nigerian banks launch into distress when it emerged that many bank managers had looted their financial institutions, through irregular and unsecured loans to themselves and cronies, or even outright stealing of depositor's funds. These actions not only plunged the entire economy into economic crisis but also caused the loss of life-savings by many customers.

Similar malfeasances were observed during the second banking crisis which began in 2008 following the global financial meltdown (reduction of capital inflows and massive capital flight) (Echebiri, 2011:52), which was compounded by gigantic frauds and unethical practices, including irregular loans and outright misappropriation of depositors funds. Most Nigerian banks were affected but the degree of exposure varied. The most implicated banks included the likes of Oceanic, Intercontinental, Bank PHB, Spring and Equitorial Bank. These banks were temporarily saved through a massive injection of public funds (about N620 Billion) by the Central Bank of Nigeria who feared a total collapse of the financial system. They were all later sold or liquidated. The consequences of the crisis on the Nigerian economy and the population were huge. Apart from the diversion of public resources to these banks, thousands of Nigerians lost their jobs and investments in the banks, thereby worsening the poverty level in the country.

All these cases discussed above clearly show that the loss of public funds required for infrastructural development, improvement in human capital and production capabilities, and health care, constitutes a roadblock to the realization of poverty reduction.

Inequality implies the dispersion of a distribution whether one is considering income, consumption or some other welfare indicators or attributes. Although conceptually distinct, income inequality is often studied as part of the broad analysis covering poverty and welfare. Thus, inequality is a broader concept than poverty because it is defined over a whole distribution. The pattern of income distribution has been of great concern to economists for a long time. Pigou (1912) and Dalton (1920), proposed a PigouDalton transfer principle. This principle opines that inequality increases when there is a transfer of income from a poorer to a richer person. Most measure of inequality in literature satisfies this principle. Furthermore, Dalton proposed the population principle of income inequality measurement, which observes that inequality measures are invariant to replications of the populations. This implies that, merging two identical distributions will not alter the level of inequality.

However, following the works of Kuznets, on the relationship between development and income inequality, many development economists have been inspired to find the major sources of income inequality. In this regard, Datt and Ravallion, proposed a method that decomposed poverty change into income redistribution, income growth and a residual component, otherwise known as the "Black box". Kakwani adopted an axiomatic approach to decompose poverty change into their growth and redistribution components. On the factors that could possibly widen or reduce income distribution in a country, Alayande (2003), decomposed income inequality in Nigeria using a regression-based approach as proposed by (Morduch and Sinclair, 2002). With 1996/1997 data, the Gini decomposition method revealed that primary and post-secondary educational attainments are important in reducing income inequality, while the number of unemployed persons in the households contributed positively to income inequality.

Baye (2005), using Shapley (1953) value for assigning entitlement in distributive analysis, assessed the within and between sector contributions to changes in poverty levels in Cameroon between 1984 and 1996. It was found that the within sector effect disproportionately accounted for increase in poverty, but the between sector contributions in both rural and semi-urban areas increase poverty. On the relevance of income inequality to economic development, efforts can be judged by the spread of researchers that have kept close focus at it since the past few decades. Specifically, the 1990s witnessed resurgence in theoretical and empirical attention by development economists to the distribution of income and wealth. This is because high level of income inequality produces unfavourable environment for economic growth and development. In many developing countries, studies have shown that income inequality had risen over the last two decades.

In Nigeria, accompanying the rapid growth that was had between 1965 and 1974 was a serious income disparity that is believed to have widened substantially. Despite past policy interventions to correct this abnormality, income inequality has increased the dimension of poverty in the country. Aigbokhan found that income inequality worsened after the Structural Adjustment Programme (SAP) of 1986. Similarly, poverty incidences were 28.1, 46.3, and 65.6 percent in 1980, 1985, 1996 respectively. Furthermore, studies have shown that a high level of income disparity exists between Nigeria's rural and urban areas (UNDP, 2000). This is largely because most rural communities depend on agriculture, while urban engage mostly in paid jobs. This lopsided development in income distribution has often times resulted in discontents, violence, corruption, hence, as part of macroeconomic objectives, government always gives equitable distribution of income a priority. This is important because income inequality is closely related to poverty and a careful study of it gives some insight into the incidence of poverty.

While economists have a theory of economic inequality, there is no theory of poverty in the conventional sense of the word. Rather, poverty theories are woven around the objects and subjects, as well as the nature of the phenomenon.

The capitalist entrepreneurial theory opines that the rather crude exploitation of the poor by means of low wages and poor conditions of services allows for a possible rise in savings among the entrepreneurial class. The resultant inequality in income could result in the preponderance of poverty among the peasant majority.

In explaining poverty and inequality, economists opine that poverty theories are woven around the objects and subjects, as well as the nature of the phenomenon. The individual attributes theory, on the other hand, posits that an individual's location in the society's hierarchy of income and wealth is presumed to be determined above all, by his motivations, attitudes and abilities.

The national-circumstantial theories identify factors such as geographical locations and natural endowments of the environment in which persons live including such other variables as unemployment, old-age, physical disabilities, etc. as culprit of poverty. The power theory recognizes the structure of political power in the society as the main determinant of the extent and distribution of poverty among the population.

The modem theoretical approach, however, considers the income dimension as the core of most poverty-related problems. To this end, poverty may arise from (a) change in average income and, (b) change in the distribution of income. Assuming a relationship between poverty line (L) and the average income of the population (Y), the poverty index will increase/decrease as L/Y increases/decreases. So, the higher average income is above the poverty line, ceteris paribus, there will be less poverty. Also, if for instance two countries with identical mean income (and poverty line, L), but with one having a wider spread of distribution of income, poverty will generally be greater in the country with higher inequality, since there will be relatively more people with incomes lower than the poverty line (L).

Unemployment in Nigeria, particularly in the form of Graduate Unemployment has become endemically pronounced in the last two decades. This situation is due primarily to upsurge in the turnout from the nation's Tertiary Institutions (Universities, Polytechnics and Colleges of Education). Not only this, it is also as a result of inelastic labour absorptive capacity of the Nigerian labour market for the service of these graduates (NISER). Unemployment and Poverty in Nigeria have attracted the attention of various categories of institutions; government, corporate bodies and individual alike. To this end, government in Nigeria over the years had embarked on a number of programmes to eradicate the twin plagues of unemployment and poverty. As such, programmes that featured in Nigeria in the past include; Directorate of Food, Roads and Rural infrastructure (DFRRI), Better Life Programme (BLP), Family Support Programme (FSP), National Directorate of Employment (NDE), Family Economic Advancement Programme (FEAP), Peoples Bank of Nigeria (PBN), Federal Urban and Mass Transit Programme, National Agricultural Land Development Authority (NALDA).

Despite the laudable programmes outlined above and the urge scarce resources devoted to poverty alleviation, the level of poverty and unemployment and the general wellbeing of many Nigerians have failed to improve. Obadan, thus referred to the situation as embarrassing paradox of poverty in the midst of plenty in Nigeria. In addition, Akinmulegun, opined that all these are as a result of poor implementation of the various programmes in the nation Nigeria. He further stressed that the programmes were ineffective due to the endemic corruption prevailing in the nation especially among the ruling class and the misappropriation of resources of the count.

While others are on a decrease since 2002, Nigerian case has been on an increase and in a geometric trend. This is presented in the table below also in a percentage form;

Table 11: Percentage of Unemployment Rate

Year	Percentage of unemployment rate (absolute)
2000	13.9
2001	13.6
2002	11.6
2003	14.8
2004	13.4
2005	11.9
2006	14.6
2007	12.7
2008	14.9
2009	19.7
2010	21.1
2011	23.9
2012	24.3

Source: IMF (www.economywatch.com)

Table 12: Graduates Unemployment Rates 2003 – 2011

Year	Rural	Urban	Total
2003	8.3	17.3	25.6
2004	12.8	25.2	38
2005	13.3	19.0	32.3
2006	13.4	18.8	32.2
2007	13.4	18.7	32.1
2008	21.7	15.8	37.5
2009	19.8	19.2	39
2010	20.7	22.8	43.5
2011	25.6	17.1	42.7

Sources: ILO 2010; The National Bureau of Statistics (NBS2010-2011) socio-economic survey of unemployment

8.   ANALYSES OF LEGAL FRAMEWORKS OF THE FIGHT AGAINST CORRUPTION IN NIGERIA

It may not be possible to recount all the laws, institutions and structures involved in the fight against corruption in Nigeria. We shall here only attempt a summary of the major laws and institutions.

The Criminal Code/Penal Code (10)

Both the Criminal Code and the Penal Code have provisions prohibiting corruption. However both codes focus on corruption in the public sector thereby neglecting the private sector which now constitutes the engine of growth in every economy. The Criminal Code provides for official corruption and judicial corruption. According to Okonkwo, offences of official corruption can be roughly divided into the offences of bribery and the offences of extortion. The offences of bribery are mainly contained in sections 98 and 116 of the Criminal Code and the elements common to both sections are as follows:

(i)   the public officer corruptly asks, receives, or obtains or agrees or attempts to receive or obtain a bribe

(ii)   The act of asking, receiving obtaining or agreeing or attempting to receive or obtain the bribe by the public officer must have been done "corruptly' and

(iii)   There should be offered, demanded or received 'any property or benefit of any kind for the public officer or any other person on account of anything already done or omitted to be done or t be afterwards done or omitted to be done by him'.

The offences of extortion by pubic officers are provided in section 404(1) a-d of the Criminal Code and involves a public servant taking advantage of his position (Colour of employment) to extort money from any person. Section 114 defines the offence of judicial corruption and a private person who offers a bribe to any judicial officer on account of anything already done or omitted to be done or to be afterwards done or omitted to be done by him in his judicial capacity is liable to fourteen years imprisonment. The provisions of the Criminal Cod on Corruption have been seriously criticized.

The criticisms include: its inability to deal effectively with both private and official corruption and its complex and difficulty worded provisions relating to corruption and kindred offences which despite their similarity are inexplicably scattered throughout the Code; and its failure to make provisions for restitution and or forfeiture of corruptly acquired property or money. The result, according to Okonkwo is the uncomfortable number of cases where the courts have felt compelled to acquit an obviously dishonest accused simply because he was charged under the wrong section.

Commenting on this situation, T.A. Aguda stated that:

> *"in so far as corruption is concerned, the Criminal Code is a completely confused piece of legislation. I say this with the greatest sense of responsibility. Many of the sections of the Criminal Code deal with various aspects of the same matter... This is a legacy of the British government in Nigeria of which, most regretfully, we have not found it possible to divest ourselves..."*

T.A. Aguda wrote this in 1983 and a number of significant legal developments have taken place since then. They include the establishment of the ICPC and EFCC which is hereby considered.

The ICPC and EFCC: The ICPC was established in 2000 by the Corrupt Practices and Other Related Offences Act (hereinafter called, The Act). Its provisions, to a large extent, addressed the inadequacies of the Criminal Code and Penal Code. The offences prohibited by the Act include accepting gratification, giving or accepting gratification through an agent, concealing offences relating to corruption, fraudulent acquisition of property, fraudulent receipt of property deliberate frustration of investigation by the Commission, making false statement or return, bribery of public office, bribery for giving assistance in regard to contracts etc.

Private persons are covered by most of the offences because the provision generally begins with 'any person who...' Also there is provision for forfeiture of gratification received by a public officer and payment of fine of not less than five times the sum or value of the gratification received. The ICPC is empowered to receive, investigate and present any report of corruption against any person. It is also empowered (amongst others) to examine the practices, systems and procedures of public bodies and direct or supervise a review where it thinks that such practices, systems or procedure aid or facilitate corruption. Officers of the body also enjoy the immunities of police officers when investigating or prosecuting cases of corruption.

One of the criticisms of the Criminal Code in respect of the offence of official corruption is the requirement for the prosecution to prove that the public officer received, or demanded the property 'corruptly'. In order to avoid this difficulty, section 53 of the ICPC Act provides that" where in any proceedings against any person for an offence under sections 8-19, it is proved that any gratification has been accepted or agreed to be accepted, obtained or attempted to be obtained".

Notwithstanding the wide range of offences covered by the Act and the enormous powers of the ICPC, Nigerians are yet to see any significant progress in the fight against corruption by the body. The Act has been criticized for the following:

a. The Act is an ex-post measure, being a legal and institutional enforcement measure designed to detect and prosecute already committed corrupt acts;

b. There is lack of commitment on the part of government to extensively expand the operation of the anti-corruption commission;

c. There is failure on the part of government to seriously incorporate the civil society in the struggle against corruption; and,

d. Failure on the part of the civil society itself to articulate its position and mobilize against corruption.

EFCC

EFCC was established by the EFCC (Establishment) Act 2002 for the investigation and prosecution of all financial Crimes including advance fee fraud, money laundering, counterfeiting, illegal charge transfers, futures market fraud, fraudulent encashment of negotiable instruments, computer credit fraud, contract scam etc. The commission is also charged with the enforcement of the following legislations-the Money Laundering Act

1995, the Advance Fee Fraud Act 1995, the Failed Banks (Recovery of Debts) and Financial Malpractices in Banks Act 1994 (as amended) the Banks and Other Financial Institutions Act 1991 (as amended), the Miscellaneous Offences Act and other laws relating to economic and financial crimes.

The definition of economic and financial crimes is very wide. It is defined as the nonviolent criminal and illicit activity committed with the objectives of earning wealth illegally either individually or in a group or organized manner thereby violating existing legislation governing the economic activities of government and its administration and includes any form of fraud, narcotic drug trafficking, money laundering, embezzlement, bribery, looting and any form of corrupt malpractices, illegal arms deal, smuggling, human trafficking and child labour, illegal oil bunkering and illegal mining, tax evasion, foreign exchange malpractice including counterfeiting of currency, theft of intellectual property and piracy, open market abuse, dumping of toxic wastes and prohibited goods etc.

The EFCC has been very active in the investigation and prosecution of past public office holders especially State governors. Examples include the investigation and prosecution of Chief Executives and other officials of banks for money laundering and other frauds. Its fight against advance fee fraud popularly called 419 has also resulted in the recovery of millions of dollars from fraudsters. The Commission has been criticized for not following due process in its activities and for being selective and partial. It has also been accused of going beyond its jurisdiction. The ICPC was created to fight corruption while the EFCC was created to wage war against financial and economic crimes. But the EFCC has taken over the function and duties of the ICPC. whatever the criticism may be, the Commission has achieved a lot in the fight against corruption in Nigeria and many Nigerians presently look up to it for better days to come in the fight against corruption.

The Code of Conduct Bureau and Tribunal Act

The code of conduct bureau and tribunal act established a bureau charged with the functions of receiving assets declarations by public officers, examining the assets declarations to ensure compliance with the requirements of the Act, taking and retaining custody of such assets declarations, receiving complaints about non-compliance with or breach of the Act and if necessary refer such complaint to the code of conduct tribunal established by section 20 of the Act. In addition, the Act contains a code of conduct for serving and retired public officers. Section 10 prohibits a public officer from asking for or accepting any property or benefit of any kind for himself or any other person on account of anything done or omitted to be done by him in the discharge of his duties. Section 7 prohibits some public officers from maintaining or operating a foreign bank account. The code of conduct tribunal is empowered to impose punishment which may include vacation of office whether elective or nominated office as the case may be; disqualification from holding any public office (whether elective or not) for a period not exceeding ten years; and seizure and forfeiture to the state of any property acquired in abuse or corruption of office. Although the code of conduct and tribunals act was enacted in 1989, the 1999 Constitution also established the code of conduct bureau as one of the federal executive bodies.

The Public Procurement Act

The Public Procurement Act No. 14 of 2007 (The Act) is another legislation aimed at guiding against corruption in Nigeria. The Act covers all aspects involved in public sector procurement including the procurement of goods and services. The Act established the National Council on Public Procurement (The Council) and the Bureau of Public Procurement (The Bureau) as the regulatory authorities responsible for the monitoring and oversight of public procurement, setting standards, harmonizing existing government policies and practices and developing legal framework and capacity for public procurement in Nigeria. There is no doubt that public procurement is one area through which billions of the public funds are looted in Nigeria. The Act thus ensures that procurement is organized and laid down methods and policies strictly followed. Section 53(1) of the Act empowers the Bureau to review and recommend for investigation any matter related to the conduct of procurement process by any Ministry or agency of government, if it considers such investigation desirable so as to detect or prevent the violation of any of the provisions of the Act.

The Role of the Legislature

The effective exercise of the oversight functions of the legislature over the activities of the executive can go a long way in exposing corrupt practices. Section 88 of the 1999 constitution empowers each House of the National Assembly to conduct an investigation into the conduct of affairs of any person, authority, ministry or government department; the disbursing or administering of moneys appropriated or to be appropriated by the National Assembly etc. One of the purposes of this investigative power is to "expose corruption, inefficiency or waste in the execution or administration of funds appropriated by the National Assembly".

The Auditor-General

There is an auditor-general for the Federation as well as for each of the states of Nigeria. He audits the public accounts of the Federation or State (as the case may be). The Auditor-General is also empowered to conduct periodic checks of all government statutory corporations, commissions, authorities, agencies including all persons and bodies established by the National Assembly or the State House of Assembly (as the case may be). It has been suggested that the Constitution ought to be amended to provide for the auditor –general's report to be made public as in some other countries. Also, in view of failure of the auditor-general of the federation and the states to audit the accounts of the federation and the states, in some years, it has been suggested that the duty to audit be made compulsory and backed by penal sanctions.

Other Laws/Institutions

Much federal and state legislation have provisions aimed at checking corruption. A good example is the recently enacted Freedom of Information Act and the local government laws of the various states. In respect of institutions, the Nigeria Police is an institution whose principal duty is to detect crime, prevent crime, investigate crime and arrest offenders for purposes of prosecution. Ordinarily, it should be at the vanguard of the fight against corruption but it has failed woefully because of its internal contradictions. As one of the most corrupt institutions in the country, it lacks the moral standing as well as the confidence of the people which is a sine qua non for any effective crime control including the fight against corruption. Finally the role of non-governmental organizations, media houses, the Civil Society groups like the Nigerian Bar Association and the Nigeria Labour Congress in the fight against corruption cannot be overemphasized.

International Conventions and Treaties

In discussing the legal framework for the fight against corruption in Nigeria, it is important also to mention the role of international conventions and treaties. Nigeria presently has a legal cooperation Treaty with the United Kingdom and this has helped a lot in apprehending fleeing offenders. Recently, the then Nigerian President Umaru Yar' Adua also made a call for a similar treaty with Germany. This call may not be unconnected with the recent allegation of bribery involving a Germany Company Siemens' and some top Nigerian officials. There is the UN Convention against Corruption which came into force on December 14, 2005. Nigeria should hasten to ratify the Convention. Under the said Convention State parties are required to criminalize corrupt activities like money-laundering, corruption, obstruction of justice etc. and to adopt legislations and administrative systems providing for extradition, mutual legal assistance, investigative cooperation, preventive and other measures.

Issues/Controversies and Suggestions

The establishment of the Independent Corrupt Practices Commission (ICPC) and the Economic and Financial Crimes Commission (EFCC) in 2000 and 2002 respectively has taken the fight against corruption in Nigeria to a higher level. The impact cannot be overemphasized as Nigeria has recorded a significant drop in the world's corruption index. Expectedly, the activities of these two bodies have been trailed by a number of issues and controversies. Let us now discuss some of these issues/controversies which we consider important and relevant to the legal framework for the fight against corruption in Nigeria.

The Power to Legislate on Corruption

As between the Federation and the State, who has the right to legislate on corruption? When the Corruption Practices and Other Related Officers Act 2000 was enacted and made to apply throughout Nigeria, many states opposed it. Consequently, the government of Ondo State instituted an action in the Supreme Court against the Attorney-General of the Federation and all the remaining thirty five states of Nigeria. Invoking the original jurisdiction of the Supreme Court, the Plaintiff prayed amongst others for a determination whether or not the Corrupt Practices and Other Related Offences Act 2000 is valid and as a law enacted by the National Assembly and in force in every state of Nigeria including Ondo State. The major contention against the Act is that since the States or local governments employ their staff, pay, promote, discipline and remove them from office, any crime arising from or incidental to their functions should be handled at the state level. To them the Anti-Corruption Act offends the principle of federation which according to Nwabueze is that:

> *An arrangement whereby powers of a government within a country are shared between national country-wide government and a number of regionalized (i.e. territorially localized) governments in such a way that each exists as a government separately and independently from the others operating directly on persons and property within its territorial area.*

In resolving the controversy, the Supreme Court held that based on section 4(2) and section 15(5) of the 1999 Constitution as well as items 60a, 67 and 68 in the Exclusive legislative List of the said Constitution, the National Assembly is competent to legislate on corruption for the entire Federation. Section 4(2) of the constitution empowers the National Assembly to make laws for the peace, order and good government of the Federal or any part thereof with respect to matters stated in the exclusive legislative list.

86

Section 15(5) of the Constitution contains one of the fundamental objectives and directive principles of state policy. The said section directs the State to abolish all corrupt practices and abuse of power. Then item 60a empowers the National Assembly to make laws for the realization of the fundamental objectives and directive principles of state policy.

Thus the National Assembly can make laws for the abolition of all corrupt practices and abuse of power. On the meaning of state under section 15(5), the Supreme Court held that it includes State governments and consequently, they too have the competence to make laws on corruption. However, where there is any conflict between the law made by the Nation al Assembly and that made by a state, the former shall prevail by virtue of section 4(5) of the Constitution. This decision by the Supreme Court has been endorsed by many commentators chiefly on the ground that the principle of federalism cannot be applied with pedantic rigour. There must be areas in which the two tiers of government must cooperate in order to achieve maximally the purpose of government. Although this decision has settled the constitutionality of the Corrupt Practices Act, a number of suits have been instituted against the Federal Government in respect of the activities of the EFCC on grounds similar to those canvassed in AG Ondo State VAG Federation and 35 others. They include AG Abia State vs. AG Federation and Ors which arose from the freezing of certain accounts of Abia State Government by the EFCC. Regrettably the Supreme Court did not pronounce on the merit of the suit as it was struck out for want of jurisdiction. The Supreme Court has also been criticized for the seeming volt face it made in AG Abia state Vs AG Federation and 2 Others wherein it declared unconstitutional the Act of the National Assembly which gave some Federal Agencies power to monitor the implementation and application of funds statutorily allocated to the Local government councils in the country on the ground that it contravened sections 7 and 162 of the 1999 Constitution.

That Act would have gone a long way in checking financial malpractices and outright embezzlement presently going on in our local councils.

The former Chairman of the Independent Corrupt Practices and Other Related Offences Commission (ICPC), Justice Mustapha Akanbi, was unsparing when he posited that former President Goodluck Jonathan's administration did not demonstrate enough seriousness in the fight against corruption. Akanbi, who was a former President of the Court of Appeal, said corruption, kidnapping and other societal ills have been on the rise and that government institutions and the judiciary remain helpless in rising to their statutory responsibilities. The retired judge said:

> Honestly, I do not see what is being done about corruption now. I ask myself these questions: Does it mean that all the governors are corruption-free? Does it mean all the legislators are corruption-free? Does it mean the judiciary is corruption free? We know that it is happening but people are not being arrested, no action is being taken and the end result is that people accept bribe with impunity now. At least, if they had taken few people to court, we would have known that something is being done. There is a general lull and the fight against corruption has gone down completely. Now, when you look at many people wanting to be governors, is it because they want to serve their people or that they want to go and chop? It is apparent that many of them want to enrich themselves because they know that when you go there you make money and become wealthy, ditto going to the legislature. Yet people are suffering; there is no development. Corruption, kidnapping and other ills of the society have gone on the ascendency. We know about Oduahgate and the billions of naira that Sanusi alleged was missing. The terrible thing is that the judiciary is not helping. The indices are that the moments are dark, the clouds have thickened, and corruption is escalating.

Constitutional lawyer, Mallam Yusuf Ali, a Senior Advocate of Nigeria (SAN), also accused Jonathan's administration of not doing anything at all to stamp out corruption. He urged Nigerians to know that corruption makes all the citizens poorer in the short and long run. His words:

> I have said this long time ago, there is no drive against corruption by the current government and that is quite obvious because the President believes that there is no corruption in Nigeria. He believes that what is going on is petty stealing. So, if he doesn't believe there is corruption, you can't hold him for not driving any anti-corruption war. If somebody doesn't believe there is a problem then he would not be obliged to look for solution.

In what looked like a confirmation of what his critics have been saying that the Federal Government has achieved little or nothing in the monumental fight against corruption, former President Jonathan recently said though politicians are thieves, they are not corrupt. He said:

> What many Nigerians refer to as corruption is actually stealing. Stealing is not the same thing as corruption, the President had said, sending many Nigerians into fits of rage that lasted for weeks. Just few days back, Jonathan confirmed his unwillingness to confront the monster called corruption just yet when, during his campaign rally in Lagos, he announced that he is not eager to jail anybody for corruption. They said they will start fighting corruption after they have crossed the bridge. And only two days ago, somebody stood in Port Harcourt, Rivers State and said he would catch people that steal and throw them in Kirikiri (Prisons). I agree that we must stop corruption but I will not do so by catching people and putting them in crates and jailing or killing them. We can't stop corruption that way.

Immunity of Certain Public Office Holders

Another issue that has generated a lot of controversy is the immunity from prosecution being enjoyed by certain public office holders Section 308 of the 1999 Constitution gives the President, Vice President, State Governors and their deputy's immunity from civil or criminal proceedings during their period of office. Under subsection 1(b) of the section they cannot be arrested or imprisoned during their period in office pursuant to the process of any court neither can any process of court be applied for or issued requiring or compelling their appearance. They can only be made nominal parties in any civil or criminal proceedings. Happily, the Supreme Court has held that this immunity does not shield the said public officers from being investigated. In Fawehimni Vs IGP, the Supreme Court held that section 308 does not grant to the officers mentioned in subsection (3) thereof immunity for policy investigation into allegations of crimes made against them. Investigation into a criminal complaint, according to the apex court, is not tantamount to instituting or bringing criminal proceedings.

It was based on this decision that the ICPC and EFCC were able to investigate serving State governors between 1999-2007 and many of them are presently being prosecuted. Yet, Nigerians seem to be still dissatisfied with the situation as many calls have been made for the removal of the immunity under section 308. Late President Umaru Yar'Adua even joined in this clarion call thereby underscoring the unpopularity of the immunity provision.

Akintola on the other hand argued that leaders have not been serious about fighting corruption. He argued that the fact that President Goodluck Jonathan has refused, despite calls from all quarters that he publicly declare his assets, is enough evidence that this administration is not interested in being transparent. What is he (President Jonathan) hiding?

He went on to posit that:

> *We know his background as a former deputy governor and vice president. I believe he is afraid that people could easily raise questions. Until we place the onus on public officers to justify their wealth, we will not get there. We should emulate the Asian countries where corruption attracts death penalty. The fight against corruption has to be taken seriously. It is the inability of our leaders to implement the law that is the problem. Those who are stealing us blind are not more than 5000. If Ghana could sacrifice 13 lives, we can afford to sacrifice them too for the rest of us to have peace. God even sacrificed his son to redeem the world.*

The truth is that, we will not be able to address the issue of corruption until, and unless the culprits that are caught are punished appropriately to serve as deterrent to others. Government catch people for corruption today and tomorrow you see them on the streets walking as free men and even being given higher responsibilities. What the Federal Government is doing is like window dressing he said. According to Agbaje:

> *The report by TI did not show any improvement. In fact it confirmed our position that corruption in the country has worsened. He argued that the present government has become prodigal, spending money as if money is going out of vogue. There is nothing about human and institutional development to sustain such huge spending. The leaving standard of Nigerians today is even worse than what it was before this government came on board. In a society where the government is not concerned about the plight of the people, but of the only few in power, what do you expect? The Economic and Financial Crimes Commission (EFCC) is not doing enough and the government is not bothered about that. The level for profligacy is higher now the oil sector is enough for TI to damn us (The Sun Editorial, 2012:7).*

Aturu adds:

> *I think that there is a problem with the TI rating and the parameters adopted. We can see that there is high level of looting going on in the country and that corruption is on the increase. For the report to have rated Nigeria 35th in the global corruption index could be because the report was based on faulty parameters or that other countries of the world are doing better in corruption than us. Certainly, there is nothing on ground to show that we are doing anything to fight corruption (The Sun Editorial, 2012:7).*

EFCC Power to Prosecute and the Role of the Attorney-General of the Federation

When the former attorney-general of the federation Mr. Aaondoakaa came into office, he reportedly issued an order directing the EFCC to hand over its files after investigation to the Attorney-General's office for prosecution. This order generated a lot of controversy as the Attorney-General was called different names and openly castigated. In fact, the well-known lawyer, late Gani Fawelhinmi issued a statement published in various dailies calling for the removal of the Attorney-General. Some questions need therefore to be answered namely.

(a) Does the EFCC have power to prosecute suspected offenders after investigation without reference to the Attorney-General as it had been doing?

(b) Have the Attorney-General supervisory powers over the EFCC?

The answer to the first question is in the affirmative. The EFCC has the power to prosecute offenders under the Act. Section 11 (1)(b) of the EFCC Act established a unit called the Legal and Prosecution Unit and section 12(2) states that one of the responsibilities of the Unit is the prosecution of offenders under the Act. There is nothing unusual with this power of prosecution by the EFCC as other bodies such as the Police, the Customs and even some Government departments also enjoy prosecutorial powers.

However, this power to prosecute is subject to the over-riding powers of the Attorney-General under Section 174 of the Constitution. That section not only gives the Attorney-General power to institute criminal proceedings against any person before any court in

Nigeria other than a court martial but also to take over and continue any such criminal proceedings that may have been instituted by any other authority or person. It also empowers the Attorney-General to discontinue any such criminal proceedings that may have been instituted by any other authority or person.

In State vs Ilori and Other, the Supreme Court held that the powers of the Attorney-General under this section are absolute and the Court cannot entertain a suit to determine whether he exercised same having regard to the public interest, the interest of justice and the need to prevent abuse of legal process. The above position shows clearly that the Attorney-General of the Federation can institute criminal proceedings after investigations by the EFCC. He can also take over and continue any criminal proceeding already instituted by the EFCC and may also discontinue such criminal proceedings. In discontinuing such criminal proceedings, the Attorney-General has no duty to give reason for the discontinuance as he is presumed to be acting on public interest. In State Vs Garba, the then Federal Court of Appeal expressed displeasure at the attitude of the High Court of Kaduna State which issued an order which had the effect of compelling the Attorney-General and the Solicitor-General respectively to appear in Court and continue with the prosecution of criminal cases even when they were not disposed.

The case against former Governor of Rivers State, Chief Dr. Peter Odili is hereby recast from a well-written petition filed before the National Judicial Commission (NJC) at the time by a UK-based Nigerian citizen, Osita Mba. In January 2007, the Economic and Financial Crimes Commission in the exercise of its statutory powers issued a report of its investigation into the finances of the Rivers State government under the then outgoing Governor Peter Odili. The "Interim Report of the EFCC on Governor Peter Odili" disclosed that "over 100 billion Naira of Rivers State funds were diverted by the Governor, and contained serious allegations of fraud, conspiracy, conversion of public funds, foreign exchange malpractice, money laundering, stealing and abuse of oath of office. Subsequently, the Rivers State Government through its Attorney-General filed an action challenging the powers of the EFCC to probe the affairs of the

State and claiming that the activities of the EFCC were prejudicial to the smooth running of the Government of Rivers State. The case was given expeditious hearing and on March 23 2007, the trial judge, Honourable Justice Ibrahim Nyaure Buba, granted all the declaratory and injunctive reliefs sought by the Plaintiff. These include a declaration that the EFCC investigations are invalid, unlawful, unconstitutional, null and void; an injunction restraining the EFCC and the other defendants from publicising the report of the investigation; and an injunction restraining the EFCC from any further action in relation to the alleged economic and financial crimes committed by Dr Odili.

In a subsequent action Dr. Odili filed against the EFCC and including the Federal Attorney General in suit no. FHC/PHC/CSI78/2007, seeking to enforce the original judgment by way of an ex parte order barring the EFCC from investigating or arresting or prosecuting him, Justice Buba held that,

> *The subsisting judgment of March 2007 by this court is binding on all parties. Therefore there is a perpetual injunction restraining the EFCC from arresting, detaining and arraigning Odili on the basis of his tenure as governor based on the purported investigation.*

Digital revolution has dissolved physical boundaries of countries around the world, making those with inadequate cybercrimes or internet related offences laws like Nigeria to be vulnerable for the commission of such crimes. Thus, legal experts always disagree on matters relating to the territorial jurisdiction for the trial of the aforesaid offences, a situation that makes the investigation and prosecution of cybercrime offences extremely difficult.

Analyses of Legal Frameworks of the Fight against Corruption outside Nigeria

Legg (2014) identifies a set of international and regional instruments/conventions that seek to inform the combat against corruption and which provides a normative legislative framework from which countries can draw as they put anti-corruption policies in place. Among the most notable of these instruments include The UN Convention against

Corruption; The AU Convention on Preventing and Combating Corruption; The OECD Anti-Bribery Convention; The SADC Anti-Bribery Convention as well as The SADC Protocol against Corruption. It is imperative to acknowledge that all the laws in the world will not stop corruption unless and until the culture within which it exists is changed. There always will be ways of getting around laws and accounting schemes.

International and Regional Instruments

Most African countries are party to a number of international and regional conventions that set out obligations to fight corruption in their respective constituencies. One of the countries in Africa that boasts of a myriad of anti-corruption policies is South Africa which has enacted domestic legislation in order to give effect to the commitments enshrined in these conventions. These conventions need to be brought into effect domestically. There are two approaches that a country can follow in making an international piece of law binding in its domestic jurisdiction, namely monism and dualism. If a country follows a monism approach, an international piece of legislation is incorporated directly into that country's legal system without a need for the country to adopt a domestic piece of legislation to give effect to the international law. In dualist countries such as South Africa, there is a difference between national law and international law. International law needs to be translated into national law, and without this translation, the international law does not apply. So there must be a piece of national law that explicitly incorporates the international law, otherwise it does not become part of national law and citizens cannot rely on it nor can judges apply it and national laws that contradict it remain in force.

The UN Convention against Corruption (UNCAC)

The United Nations Convention against Corruption (UNCAC) was ratified by South Africa in 2004 and came into force in 2005. South Africa is one of 168 parties to the convention, which means that it accepts the terms of the convention and is legally bound by its provisions. Under UNCAC, South Africa is also obliged to help other parties to prevent and fight corruption by providing technical assistance if necessary. Some of the key features of the UNCAC are the requirements to take decisive action to:

- Prevent corruption
- Criminalize corruption
- Co-operate with other countries in the fight against corruption, and
- Recover assets corruptly acquired.

These are not going to happen by themselves, says the UNCAC – parties must ensure that certain steps and processes are in place so that everybody can get involved. These requirements include the promotion of active participation of individuals and groups, including civil society and community-based organizations (CBOs), in the prevention of and fight against corruption; codes or standards of conduct for public officials; and appropriate training so that they can perform their functions effectively and honestly. These anti-corruption policies must comply with the rule of law, and foster integrity, transparency and accountability; Whistle-blowers are also covered under the convention, which states that parties should consider incorporating measures into their domestic legal systems to provide protection against unjustified treatment of persons who report corruption in good faith. South Africa's obligations in terms of this convention find expression in domestic legislation such as the Prevention and Combatting of Corrupt Activities Act; the Prevention of Organized Crime Act; the Protected Disclosures Act (also known as the Whistle-blowing Act); and the Criminal Procedure Act, among others.

The AU Convention against Corruption

The African Union Convention on Preventing and Combating Corruption was adopted in 2003 and came into force in 2005. In 2004 South Africa signed the convention and ratified it in 2005. It has a number of provisions similar to those of the UN Convention against Corruption. The AU convention requires signatories to establish, maintain and strengthen independent, national anti-corruption authorities or agencies.

The OECD Anti-Corruption Convention

The Organization for Economic Co-operation and Development's Anti-bribery Convention establishes legally binding standards to criminalize bribery of foreign public officials in international business transactions. Under the OECD convention, parties must take measures to establish that, under their own laws, it's a criminal offence for any person to bribe a foreign public official to obtain an improper benefit in international business. Parties must ensure that such action is punishable.

The SADC Protocol against Corruption

The Southern African Development Community's Protocol against Corruption was adopted by heads of state at the August 2001 summit in Malawi. This was the first sub-regional anti-corruption treaty in Africa. The SADC Protocol against Corruption provides for the prevention, detection and punishment of corruption. It also covers co-operation between states, and corruption in both the public and private sectors. The protocol recognizes that demonstrable political will and leadership are essential in the fight against corruption. It affirms the need to garner public support for initiatives to combat corruption. Given the gravity with which corruption is treated in most African countries, most of these countries have enacted domestic legislation in order to give effect to the commitments enshrined in these conventions. However, compliance with the dictates of these provisions is another thing, as it has become common for high-ranking public servants to be involved in corrupt practices.

9.   CURBING CORRUPTION IN NIGERIA

Pessimistic view

Those with a pessimistic outlook will say "nothing much" and the matter is not worth the bother. Since the top leaders, key politicians and those in power, in collusion with leading international firms and prominent local business people are involved, and are reaping huge benefits from the system, chances of bringing about change appear remote. The pessimists point out that even in a country like Britain, it has taken over a hundred years to bring corruption under control. They also note the lack of substantive progress in anti-corruption drives that are underway in many Asian countries. One country, for example, has launched a major campaign for nearly a decade, but results achieved have fallen far short of expectations. The top leaders in this country have come out strongly against corruption in their public statements on many occasions, considering it a matter of the highest national priority and concern. It is also reported that 35,084 cases of official graft and embezzlement were investigated in the country in 1998, out of which action was taken in 26,834 cases.

In addition, several prominent figures from the party, government, and the business community were arrested and persecuted. But the problem remains far from being resolved, and the country's leaders would be the first to admit this. Thus, the Prime Minister has designated fighting corruption as one of the four overriding national objectives in the country's development agenda for the coming years. While campaigns against corruption have not met with much success, there have been worrisome developments on this front that make the situation appear more hopeless. In many countries, corruption has now reached new heights where rules and regulations are increasingly looked upon by public officials as a means to augment their low salaries. New rules are invoked and existing rules changed solely to generate income for themselves. Bribery and extortion have become institutionalized and take forms such as open requests for contributions and forced sale to the general public of unwanted and unnecessary articles at high markup prices as a means to raise revenue. A basic difficulty with systemic corruption is that when the majority of people operate under such a system, individuals have no incentive to try to change it or to refrain from taking part in it even if everyone would be better off if there were no corruption. So people become resigned and try to make the best of a bad situation and to get on with their lives. Why bother changing something that can't be changed? Why bang your head against a wall? Why entertain a buffalo with harp music? Nothing lasts forever anyway, and so on, are the type of attitudes that prevail in such a society.

Optimistic view

But not everybody agrees that endemic corruption is in the nature of things and the unenviable lot of low income countries. These more optimistic people point out that there are developing countries in the world, such as Botswana and Chile that, at present, have less bribery than many industrialized countries. They note that developing economies like Hong Kong, China and Singapore have been able to transform themselves from being very corrupt to relatively clean within a reasonably short period of time. They also point to serious efforts at market reforms and development of democratic institutions that are taking place in many developing countries which everybody knows would reduce opportunities for economic rent and, thus, benefits to be derived from corruption. They are encouraged by many top leaders in the Asia and Pacific region that openly discuss corruption in their countries, freely admit that it is imposing a severe strain on the social and moral fabric of their communities, that it is destroying their institutions, and hence recognize it as a critical problem that must be urgently addressed.

Finally, the optimists also point out that campaigns against poverty, hunger, disease and injustice have been going on for decades and the fact that they have yet to yield satisfactory results in many parts of the world, does not mean that such efforts should cease. The fight against corruption, they say, should be viewed in the same light. No one claims it can be eliminated. But they believe it can and should be checked and brought under control so that the bad effects are minimized.

Remedial measures

Some ideas and suggestions that have been put forward by the members of the optimistic camp to fight corruption are as follows:

Leadership: For proper house cleaning and repairs, it is a good idea to begin by fixing the roof. Hence, many authors, including Professor Syed Hussein Alatas of Malaysia, a noted authority on corruption, are of the view that the leadership in a country has a key role to play in combating corruption. It is an Asian tradition to hold leaders and those in authority in high regard and esteem. Hence the top leadership must set a good example with respect to honesty, integrity and capacity for hard work. Since fighting corruption will involve taking difficult decisions, the leadership must also display firmness, political will and commitment to carry out the required reforms. But honest and dedicated leaders are a necessary, but not a sufficient, condition to counter corruption. Several other conditions need to be satisfied.

Credibility: Credibility is one of them. For success, the offenders both on the demand and supply side of a corrupt deal must be convinced that the government is serious about fighting corruption. One suggestion towards this end is to "fry some big fish", that is to publicly try and punish some well-known corrupt people in the country. Some highly publicized trials and convictions of important officials and businessmen on charges of corruption have taken place in several Asian countries. However, since allegations of corruption are often used to discredit political opponents, the suggestion is further made that the fish that is fried should preferably be from your own pond.

Involving people: A publicity campaign to create greater awareness on the adverse effects of corruption and a clear and unequivocal official pronouncement on the desirability to bring it under control would be helpful. Ordinary citizens have a lot of firsthand experience with corruption, they are a good source of information and their help and cooperation should be solicited for the successful launch of an anti-corruption drive. Once people are convinced that a sincere and genuine effort to combat corruption is underway, they will respond and extend their full cooperation in resolving the problem. Just a little opening up and providing opportunities for them to express their views on the matter will bring forth an outpouring of information, ideas and suggestions that will be beyond anyone's imagination.

Responsible press: A responsible press to gather, analyze, organize, present and disseminate information is considered vital to create greater public awareness and to provide the momentum for undertaking reforms to overcome corruption. Secretiveness has been a key factor that has enabled public officials and politicians to get away with corruption. A responsible and an investigative press has played an important role in many countries, both developed and developing, in exposing misconduct as well as in serving as a watchdog to limit corruption and preventing it from getting out of hand. The press has not always acted in a responsible manner, and like everything else in this world, it is not perfect. Nevertheless, its power to limit misconduct and improper behaviour should not be underestimated.

Oversight bodies: Views on the effectiveness of anti-corruption oversight or watchdog bodies are mixed. There are instances where they have proved useful. For example, the Independent Commission Against Corruption in Hong Kong, China, and similar institutions in Botswana, Chile, Malaysia and Singapore are regarded as having done a good job. However, in surveys and interviews of public officials and members of civil society organizations, most respondents do not have a high opinion of them. The prevailing view is that for such bodies to be effective, they have to be created in a political atmosphere where leaders are honest, civil servants are insulated from political interference, and better incentives are provided to discourage corruption. Otherwise, the oversight bodies will be rendered useless or worse, misused for political gain. An unwelcome situation can then arise and the country may have to appoint a watchdog to watch over the watchdog body.

Improving institutions: This is a very large area and only brief mention can be made of the relevant issues. It involves such things as improving the legal framework; smoother, less time-consuming and less burdensome ways to conduct business in the functioning of law courts and in the administration of justice; promoting efficiency of the police force;

101

strengthening the auditor general's office; and appointment of a responsible inspector general empowered to investigate and prosecute corruption.

To fight corruption effectively requires taking the following steps:

1. Exposing the problem, which is the business of the media, and

2. Appointing an aggressive Attorney-General,

3. Punishing the corrupt for all to see that crime does not pay. No exceptions to the rule of law.

The first step has been stymied by the fact that the media in much is controlled by the state. Only 8 African countries have a free media. The state uses the media to control the flow of information and to conceal corruption and wrong-doing. When intrepid journalists expose them, they are brutally assaulted by security forces – or worse.

On Feb 22, 1998, armed soldiers invaded the Ondo State television station, ransacked the editorial offices and took away the evening bulletins which included accounts of the assault two days earlier on the station's media managers, Dunni Fagbayiyo and Tunde Yusuff. Five days later, unidentified gunmen killed Tunde Oladepo, a senior editor of The Guardian, after breaking into his Ogun State home. "He was shot to death in front of his wife and children. The murderers stayed in the house for 30 minutes after shooting him to make sure the journalist was dead".

Attacks on the media continued, even under the "democratic" regimes. On April 4, 2000, nine armed members of the dreaded State Security Service (SSS) invaded This Day newspaper offices in Abuja, claiming they were looking for "subversive and incriminating documents". Earlier on Jan 19, 2000, 50 police raided the international press center in Lagos with guns drawn, demanding computer files and arresting journalists on suspected charges of terrorism. Obviously, control of the media must be wrestled out of the hands of the state if the fight against corruption is to succeed.

Second, an aggressive Attorney-General or anti-corruption czar should be appointed and given the powers of prosecution. Such an Attorney-General or czar must be protected by the President himself or, failing that, by western donors. Third, combating corruption will require reforming the judicial system. Only an independent judiciary can establish the rule of law and prosecute corrupt government officials. As we have seen, state governors loot with impunity because the corrupt are seldom punished.

Further measures can be taken as well in the fight against corruption.
The pervasive array of state controls which breed corruption and malpractices must be removed. It entails the removal of controls on prices, exchange rates, imports, exports, rents, and others. These controls did not exist in Africa's own indigenous economic system in the first place. Such measures would liberalize the economy, by taking economic power out of the hands of the state and giving it back to the people where it rightly belongs. Incidentally, this is partly what Structural Adjustment Programs are intended to do. An independent central bank is also vital, as can be discerned from the following quote:

"Swiss judicial authorities have opened an inquiry into alleged money laundering and participation in a criminal organization involving Nigeria's late leader Sani Abacha and his entourage. Abacha, his eldest son Muhammed Sani Abacha, his widow Mariam and brother Abdulkadir, are among those accused by Nigeria's elected government of having "systematically plundered" the country's central bank, a Swiss statement said earlier in October, 1999. A Geneva lawyer representing the Nigerian Government alleges Abacha and his entourage diverted $2.2 billion from the Central Bank alone".

It is recommended that rotating governors of central banks in a region, say West Africa; which would help enhance the "independence" of the central bank. Further, to help combat corruption effectively, it might be best to appoint a non-national (a Westerner or African) to head the anti-corruption units. For example, a Ghanaian may be appointed in Nigeria and a Nigerian in Kenya. The reason is that quite often non-national Africans do perform well when pulled out of their socio-cultural environment since they are not burdened by a myriad of social obligations. A Ghanaian is not Yoruba or Igbo and therefore cannot be expected to grant special tribal favors to a corrupt Yoruba politician.

Lessons must be drawn from anti-corruption efforts in other African countries. African governments set up anti-corruption commissions with no teeth to prosecute the corrupt. And when they snoop too close, they are shut down. Such was the case of Richard Leakey, appointed by Kenya's expresident Daniel arap Moi in July 1999 to head the civil service in an effort to eradicate corruption. But when he pried too close, he was sacked six months later. The next anti-corruption czar, John Githongo, appointed in 2001 by the new president, Mwai Kibaki, did not fare better. When he fingered thieving ministers, threats were made on his life and he fled to Britain in 2005.

The rare case of success in the fight against corruption comes from South Africa. There President Thabo Mbeki swung into action and established "The Scorpions," South Africa's elite anti-corruption unit, which had pursued "bigger fish" – senior members of the ruling party, the African National Congress (ANC). The Scorpions went after Jacob Zuma, the deputy president and the most likely successor to President Mbeki, who was "accused of (and denies) asking for 500,000 rand (or $68,000) from a foreign arms company, Thales, to protect it from a probe into alleged kickbacks". Other senior government officials also felt the sting of The Scorpions: Tony Yengeni, chief whip of the African National Congress was jailed in 2003 as was Winnie Madikizela-Mandela, former wife of Nelson Mandela. The conviction of Yengeni centered on his purchase of a luxury sport utility vehicle that was sold to him at a steep discount by a defense contractor. The contractor, European Aeronautic Defense and Space Co., eventually won a contract to build radar systems as part of a $6 billion package of weapons purchases made by the government in 2001.

Mrs. Madikizela-Mandela, the president of the ANC's Women's League and member of Parliament, was convicted of defrauding a bank of more than $103,000. She was still a member of parliament when she was jailed. She was involved in a scheme in which a codefendant obtained personal loans for fictitious Women's League employees by using her name and letterhead to support the fraudulent loan applications. Mrs. Madikizela-Mandela publicly denied the bank fraud charges. In an interview with the City Press newspaper, "she acknowledged financial problems, but said the investigation was inspired by her rivals within the A.N.C. She had been one of Mr. Mbeki's most vocal critics, assailing him for questioning whether H.I.V. causes AIDS and condemning the government for promoting conservative economic policies that she says neglect the poor. "One can safely conclude that the campaign is being waged within my organization," Mrs. Madikizela-Mandela said:

"The Scorpions report an impressive conviction rate of 85 percent and enjoy huge popular support. And the secret of their success?, Cases of graft are known about largely because the police, newspapers and political parties are free to unearth them. The national prosecuting authority now has over 3,500 staff and fast-rising budget worth 950 million rand (or $129 million) in 2003. In July 2003, Mr. Mbeki authorized a probe into 285 cases of fraud in the department of justice and the courts and police are broadly free of political meddling. The president says of his deputy's troubles that the 'law must run its course '".

Again, it is worth recounting the ingredient of this successful campaign: freedom to unearth cases of corruption (exposure), prosecuting the corrupt for all to see and providing funds and staff to the prosecuting authority. These ingredients are woefully lacking in Nigeria. If Nigerian leaders want to be popular with their people, they should establish "The Scorpions" or "Black Mambas" in the country.

Generally, the following must be done to effectively combat corruption in Nigeria
Because of its destructive propensity, corruption must be deterred in our society. Although, it is difficult but can still be fought to an insignificant level of existence. Successive governments have initiated various strategies aimed at fighting corruption such as War Against Indiscipline (WAI), Independent Corrupt Practices and Other Related Offences (ICPC), Economic and Financial Crimes Commission (EFCC) among others, yet, corruption continues unabated. It thrives because most of the institutions

established to combat corruption are not either constitutionally, legally, organizationally nor financially empower to be independent in a way to act without external influence in discharging their duties. To genuinely war against corruption, the necessary institutions should be made effective and independent.

Importantly, there must be political commitment, will and capacity on the part of the leaders. Legal and institutional frameworks are not enough but appropriate laws are to be enacted to empower them to prosecute law breakers. Corruption cannot be fought by those leaders who ascended their position through corrupt practices and still thrive in corruption while in office. Also, corrupt practice must be punished at all levels. Corruption can only be fought effectively when no one is speared. Anybody caught in the act must face the wrought of law, irrespective of his position in the government or status in the society. A "socio-psycho" mechanism for combating corruption should be developed by the civil society. Socio-psycho mechanism is the system of rejecting corrupt people and their assistance in the society. It is high time we stopped respecting their wealth and personality, every donation and form of assistance from them should be rejected. Nobody should be ready to be identified with them so that they can suffer identity crisis even within their primordial constituency. It is also reasonable that government should genuinely alleviate poverty to make this mechanism work.

Another important factor that should be considered in the fight against corruption is the immunity clause. The immunity clause ample judiciary and other anti-graft agencies to work effectively. Because they do not have power to probe, question or sanction some of the political office holders. The clause itself is an attractive object of corruption or to corrupt practices by those that are concerned. Once they know they have become untouchable, then, the tendency to act corruptly while in office becomes so high. Hence, the immunity clause must be expunged from the constitution as a matter of emphasis and urgency.

Unfortunately, the institutions set up by the Federal Government to fight corruption cannot be truly independent e.g. ICPC, EFCC and others. This is because they are agents of federal government. Therefore, they become tools in the hands of such level of government either to witch-hunt opponents or silent critics and mostly the innocent civil servants, who are earnestly waiting to get their entitlement.

Also, the legislature needs to be alive to their oversight functions especially at state level. They should not create unnecessary rapport of conspiracy that will further amputate them from checking the excesses of the executive. Although, a good relationship between the two is important to facilitate effective performance, but a relationship that consolidate democracy and not the one that strengthens patronage.

There must be strict observance of separation of power by the three arms of government. The necessary institutions created for anti-corruption must be adequately funded, independent and their capacity fully enhanced.

Religious, educational and marriage institutions are also to be strengthened for role performance. This is because fundamentally corruption is in the heart and so requires moral approach to deal with it; this moral approach involves education, enlightenment and orientation geared towards attitudinal change of the people, which can be effectively carried out by these institutions.

There should be anti-corruption unit that will be independent in all departments of government ministries, agencies and parastatals. And the anti-corruption should not only focus on fiscal accountability, it should also deal with managerial accountability to ensure that managers utilize public resources and eliminate wastage.

Lastly, electoral corruption is the worst of them all because it gives way to other corrupt practices. There should be strict penalty, if it is possible life imprisonment, for whoever is caught in electoral corruption.

What the International Community Can Do to Help

It would be wrong to leave you with the impression that corruption alone is the major scourge afflicting Nigeria. In the grips of a constitutional crisis, torn by sectarianism, North-South divide over claims to the presidency, religious and ethnic rivalries and communal violence, the country teeters on the brink of disintegration. These broader issues are best handled are best handled in a "sovereign national conference." This political vehicle was successfully used by Benin in 1991 and South Africa in 1994 (the Convention for a Democratic South Africa – CODESA) to chart a new democratic political dispensation for their respective countries. To help Nigeria in its efforts to tackle its problems, the U.S. government could do any of the following:

Help tighten international regulations against money-laundering, especially in developing countries in Asia, which now seem to be the destination point of looted funds.

Help persuade the Nigerian government to place a certain percentage of oil revenues into an offshore escrow account, to be managed by an independent body for the benefit of the people in the Niger Delta.

BIBLIOGRAPHY

Adekunle, F. (1991) *Illustrations of Types, Patterns and Avenues of Corruption in Nigeria: A Typology, Perspectives or Corruption and other Economic Crimes in Nigeria*, Lagos: Federal Ministry of Justice.

Aigbokhan, B. (1997) *Poverty Alleviation in Nigeria: Some Macroeconomic Issues.* Nigerian Economic Society's Annual Conference Proceedings, Ibadan

Ajie, H.A. & Oyegun, G. (2015). Corruption and Economic Growth in Nigeria: An Empirical Analysis 1996-2013. *European Journal of Business and Management*, 7(5):224-243

Akinmulegun, S.O. (2014). Unemployment and Poverty Paradigm in Nigeria: Challenges and Prospect. *International Journal of Management and Administrative Sciences*, 2(3):16-23

Alemann, U.V. (1995) *Corruption in Germany. The debate in politics and political science.* Paper prepared for the IX Jornadas de Filosofía Práctica organized by the Facultat de Dret Universitat Pompeu Fabra Barcelona May 25 and 26, 1995 at Tossa de Mar

Alemika, E., Sha, D.P., Obe, A.O., Ya'u, Y.Z. & Adeniyi. S. (2015). *Corruption and Poverty in Nigeria*: A Report. Action Aid Nigeria

Ameh, J. & Oladimeji, R. (2014). *Corruption Stalls Nigeria's War Against Boko Haram-US.* Retrieved from http://www.punchng.com/news/corruption-stalls-nigerias-war-against-bharam-us/

Anaro, B. (January 22, 2012). Africa: The Country's Strife Highlights Africa's Investment Risks, *AllAfrica.com*

Awojobi, O.N. (2014). Corruption and Underdevelopment in Africa: A Discourse Approach. *International Journal of Economics, Commerce and Management*, 2(10): 1-14

Ayittey, G.B. (1998). *Nigeria's Struggle with Corruption.* Available online at http://www.freemedia.at/wpfr/Africa/nigeria.htm

Baye, P.M. (2005) *Structure of sectoral Decomposition of Aggregate Poverty changes in Cameroon.* Paper presented at The International Conference on Shared Growth in Africa, Accra, Ghana (July)

Begovic, B. (2005). *Corruption: Concepts, Types, Causes, and Consequences*. Washington: Center for International Private Enterprise

CASAC (2011), *Corruption: Towards a Comprehensive Societal Response*, available at http://www.casac.org.za/wpcontent/uploads/2011/03/corruptionfullreport.pdf

Chetwynd, E. (2003). *Corruption and Poverty: A Review of Recent Literature* (Final Report), Management Systems International, Washington, January 2003

Echebiri, Ray. (2011). *Rage of the Risk God: Reportage of the Lamido Sanusi Banking Reforms*, Lagos, Rayfields Communication Limited

Ekeh, P.P. (1975). Colonialism and the Two Publics: A Theoretical Statement. *Comparative Studies in Society and History*, 17(1): 91-112

Eme, O.I.(2010) "Corruption in Nigerian Government Institutions: A case of Police Equipment Fund, *Journal of Liberal Studies, University of Nigeria, Nsukka*, Pp. 440-458.

Ganahl, J.P. (2013). *Corruption, Good Governance, and the African State: A Critical Analysis of the Political-Economic Foundations of Corruption in Sub-Saharan Africa*. Deutsche: Potsdam University Press

Holmes, Leslie (2006) *Rotten State? Corruption, Post-Communism, and Neoliberalism*. Durham London: Duke University Press.

Igbuzor, O. (2008). *Strategies for Winning The Anti-Corruption War in Nigeria*. Action Aid Nigeria Briefing Paper No. 2

Iyanda, D.O. (2012). Corruption: Definitions, Theories and Concepts. *Arabian Journal of Business and Management Review*, 2(4): 37-45

Javaid, U. (2010). Corruption and Its Deep Impact on Good Governance in Pakistan. *Pakistan Economic and Social Revi*ew. 48(1):123-134

Kalu, U. (January 21, 2012). Sleazy Details from House of Reps Subsidy Probe, *The Vanguard Newspaper*

Khan, M.M. (n.d.). *Political and Administrative Corruption: Concepts, Comparative Experiences and Bangladesh Case*. Being a paper prepared for Transparency International-Bangladesh Chapter.

Langseth, P. (1999). *Prevention: An Effective Tool to Reduce Corruption.* Being a paper presented at the ISPAC conference on Responding to the Challenge of Corruption, 19 November 1999, Milan

Legg, A. (2013). *Meeting the challenge of bribery and corruption in Africa.* Available at http://www.risk.net/operational-risk-andregulation/opinion/2309455/meeting-the-challenge-ofbribery-and-corruption-in-africa (Accessed on 19 January 2014).

Liverpool-Tasie, S. (2010). *A Review of Fertilizer Policy Issues in Nigeria*, Nigeria Strategy Support Program (NSSP) NSSP Working Paper No. 0019 October 2010

Mapuva, J. (2014). The Debilitating Impact of Corruption on Democracy and Good Governance: A Critical Analysis. *International Journal of Political Science and Development*, 2(8):164-174

Merat, J. & Roth, D. (2008) *Effectivity of Institutions in the Fight against Corruption: the Strategy of Transparency Pacts in Colombia.* Mimeo.

Mohammed, U. (2013). Corruption in Nigeria: A Challenge to Sustainable Development in the Fourth Republic. *European Scientific Journal.* 9:118-137.

Myint, U. (2000). Corruption: Causes, Consequences and Cures. Asia-Pacific Development Journal. 7(2):33-58

Nwakwo, O. (2014). Impact of Corruption on Economic Growth in Nigeria. *Mediterranean Journal of Social Science*, 5(6):41-46

Odufowokan, D. (February 2, 2015), Corruption: Will 2015 elections bring respite? *The Nation Newspaper.*

Ogannah, A. (January 6, 2015), Presidential Election: Corruption is the big issue, *Daily Pilot Newspaper.*

Ogunbiyi, T. (October 20, 2014). Acting Together Against Poverty, *The Punch Newspaper*

Ogundiya, I.S. (2009). Political Corruption in Nigeria: Theoretical Perspectives and Some Explanations. *Anthropologist*, 11(4):281-29

Okolo, P.O. & Akpokighe, O.R. (2014). Corruption in Nigeria: The Possible Way Out. *Global Journal of Human-Social Science: F Political Science*, 14(7):31-38

111

Olaleye, O. & Akosile, A. (December 6, 2012), Transparency International Ranks Nigeria 35th most Corrupt Nation, This *Day Newspaper*.

Olu, A. (2014). *How Corruption Contributes to Poverty*. Being paper presented at the International Conference on Development of Social Enterprise and Social Business for Eradication of Extreme Poverty and Street Begging, holding at Chittagong, Bangladesh, December 19-20, 2014

Omotoye, R. (n.d). Corruption and Underdevelopment: The Nigerian Experience. *LUMINA*, 22(1):1-13

Osahon, S. & Osarobo, A.K. (2011). Poverty and Income Inequality in Nigeria: An Empirical Assessment. *JORIND* 9(2):447-456

Osimen, G.U., Adenegan, T.S. & Balogun, A. (2013). An Assessment of Corruption in the Public Sector in Nigeria: A Study of Akure South Local Government Area, Ondo State. *Canadian Social Science*, 9(5):87-97

Pedersen, K.H. & Johannsen, L. (2008) *Corruption: Commonality, causes and consciences. Comparing 15 ex-communist countries*. Paper prepared for the 13th NISPAcee Annual Conference May 19-21 in Moscow, Russia

Persson, T. Guido, T. & Francesco, T. (2003). Electoral Rules and Corruption. *Journal of the European Economic Association*, 1(4):958-989.

Richard, A.O. & Eme, O.I. (2015). Analyses of Legal Frameworks for Fighting Corruption in Nigeria: Problems and Challenges. *Arabian Journal of Business and Management Review*, 5(3):1-33

Santosh, H. (2011). *Effect of Corruption on Good Governance, First CIPS Foundation Day Lecture*, P1, accessed at http://www.cips.org.in/public-sector-systems-government-innovations/documents/NS-Hegde_CIPSFDL_ed20May11.pdf

Sela-i-Martin, X. and Subramanian, A. (2008). Addressing the Natural resources Curse: An Illustration from Nigeria, in Collier, Paul, C.C. Soludo and C. Pattillo (eds), *Economic Policy Options for a Prosperous Nigeria*. New York: Palgrave Macmillan

Seteolu, D. (2005). Historical Trajectories of Elections in Nigeria: The State, Political Elite and Electoral Politics. In: Godwin Onu and Abubakar Momoh (Eds.): *Elections and Democratic Consolidation in Nigeria*. Lagos: Triad Associates

Skogan, W.G. & Meares, T.L. (2004). Lawful Policing. *Annals AAPSS*, 5:66–83.

The Corrupt Practices and Other Related Offences Act 2000

The Sunday Sun Editorial (December 7, 2012). Nigeria's Dismal Corruption Ranking. *Sunday Sun Newspaper*

TI UK (2009) *Typology of defense corruption.* Available at http://hdl.handle.net/1765/10772

Tolu, L. & Ogunro, K.V. (2012). Combating Corruption in Nigeria. *International Journal of Academic Research in Economics and Management Sciences*, 1(4):1-7

Triesman, D. (1998). *The Causes of Corruption: A Cross-National Study.* Los Angeles: University of California

Umutoniwawo, R. (2012). *Impact of Corruption on Democratic Governance in Africa: The Case of Central Africa.* Being a paper presentation at International Conference on Democratic Governance: Challenges in Africa and Asia, Philadelphia, USA, 07-09 August, 2012.

United Nations Development Programme (UNDP) (2000) *Nigeria: Common Country Assessment.* March, pp. 68.

United States Institute of Peace (2010). *Study Guide Series on Peace and Conflict: Governance, Corruption, and Conflict.* Washington: USIP

Uslaner, E. (2007). Corruption and the Inequality Trap in Africa. *Afro Barometer.* Working paper No. 69.

Vargas-Hernandez, J.G. (n.d.). The Multiple Faces of Corruption: Typology, Forms and Levels. Not Available.

World Bank (1997). Helping Countries Combat Corruption: The Role of the World Bank, *Poverty Reduction and Economic Management Network*, September 1997.

World Bank (2014). *Nigerian Economic Report*, Washington D. C, No. 2, July.

www.ingramcontent.com/pod-product-compliance
Lightning Source LLC
Chambersburg PA
CBHW020541290526
45786CB00002B/982